One day by the Thames

GARETH PRICE

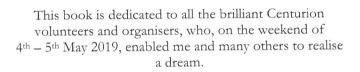

This book is dedicated to all the brilliant Centurion volunteers and organisers, who, on the weekend of 4th – 5th May 2019, enabled me and many others to realise a dream.

CONTENTS

	Introduction	*i*
1	One task	1
2	Thanks to Ray	6
3	The London Stone	9
4	Millennium Falcon	14
5	What happens next?	19
6	An Odyssean education	24
7	A different world	30
8	Alan John Price	35
9	A slide of Soreen	43
10	A mean streak	49
11	Walking like Frankenstein	53
12	Kintsugi	58
13	Performance is emotional	65
14	Aftermath	71
	Stories from other runners and volunteers	77
	Thank you	83
	References	86

INTRODUCTION

Completing the Thames Path 100 mile race was the culmination of many chapters of my life, not just running. Almost immediately after the race had finished, I felt compelled to write things down, to tell the story of why and where I ended up doing it, as well as how.

Many people probably find the idea of trying to run all day and all night a kind of madness, an addiction almost - something they would be unlikely to contemplate themselves. This book is partly an attempt to try and answer their questions about why, and to uncover some of the motivations and life experiences that drove me to do it.

But I also believe there are those out there who are open to running a long way too, who might be converted to the idea.

In the two years leading up to the race I was hungry for knowledge about ultra running. I learnt it involves any race over 26.2 miles, that although the idea seems challenging, ultra runners normally go slower, take a lot of walking 'breaks', and are careful to eat and drink enough. I sought out all the books I could lay my hands on. Alongside training guides (1), many first-hand accounts were written by people based in the States, super human types who were either up near the front of races or winning them (2). Other books focused on the deep suffering endured in tough, difficult to enter European races like the Sparthalon (3) or Ultra-Trail du Mont Blanc (4).

They were all inspirational, but while I was training for my first

100 miler, it felt like I was missing a point of view from the middle of the pack in a UK race, an account that showed how accessible and exhilarating ultras can be for normal people who make mistakes, as well as uber athletic types.

So, 'One day by the Thames' aims to fill that gap for others who may follow. It's about my first-hand experience as a 100 mile competitor – the ups and downs in the build-up, how amazing it can be to just keep going. If one person reading it is inspired and tries a longer race for themselves, I'll consider that mission accomplished. Ultra runners come in all shapes and sizes, and we quickly learn, never look at someone and second guess whether they'll be able to do it or not; we're all more capable than we think.

I hope capturing a flicker of our collective experience can also serve as a tribute to the happy few, the band of brothers and sisters who were there running the Thames alongside me; and to the Centurion volunteers and organisers, who, running with us in spirit, put a monster shift in, and selflessly did all the hours, without getting any of the glory…

1 ONE TASK

It's just after midnight and I'm striding uphill in the middle of Whitchurch-on-Thames finishing a blueberry muesli bar. The only sound is the rhythmic scrunch of my running shoes on the surface of the road. The sleepy south Oxfordshire town is well off the beaten track at the best of times; now it's all shut up for the night and no-one else is around.

The temperature is close to freezing, encouraging me to get a move on. I'm dressed in a long-sleeved tee-shirt, fleece, waterproof, hat and gloves, and bamboo leggings with shorts over the top. I'm still shivering a bit though and need to get warm again after stopping at the aid station.

It was snug in the village hall and I helped myself from the kid's party style buffet - cocktail sausages and crisps, grapes and jelly babies. There was a welcome treat when one of the volunteers gave me some of her hot chocolate. Walking out I told them - 'this has been my favourite aid station!' Another runner sarcastically countered 'he says that every time!' I recognised him – Stephen Cousins from Film My Run on YouTube (5).

Back outside, beginning what seems like a crucial part of

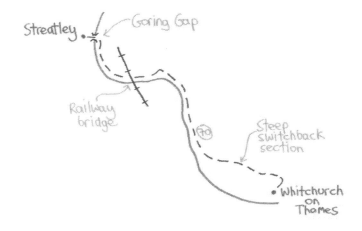

the race 67 miles in, I'm happier than I could have imagined. I've had a tough time in the build-up, worrying about all the different things that could go wrong, but now there's the hint of a smile below the surface, the possibility I may be buzzing.

The Thames Path 100 is organised by Centurion Running (6) and has a simple premise. As Jasmin Paris said after winning the 2019 Spine Race, we 'have one task' – run, walk or crawl from A to B. For us this means following the river from Richmond to Oxford within 28 hours. Make it to Oxford within the time cut off and we earn a '100 Miles Finisher' belt buckle. Do it within 24 hours and we get the coveted '100 Miles One Day' buckle.

A few minutes ago, I said goodbye to my friend Laura who has generously accompanied me as a 'pacer' for the 9 mile leg from Reading, helping me get through the first part of the night. Although I was dreading being back on my own, I realise I'm ok about it – there's nothing else to worry about apart from making progress as fast as possible.

The next major landmark is Goring Gap – a narrowing of the Thames Valley where, tens of thousands of years ago, a sheet of ice blocked the river's route to the North Sea, forcing it to cut a new route south through a weak spot between the Chilterns and the Berkshire Downs (7). Here four miles ahead, in the village of Streatley on the left side of the 'Gap', is aid station nine; that's my goal.

Up at the top of the hill, I adopt a business-like approach, determined to get to Streatley in less than an hour. I start jogging along a narrow road and catch a few people up.

Through a gate and we're on rough terrain again - a sudden switchback section with steps down a very steep slope. Our journey has been mainly flat but not right now as we negotiate this loop away from the river. I checked out the route in daylight a few weeks back so I'm ready for this, or at least think I am. I break into an accidental run halfway down and as my momentum builds, my legs start to speed up and accelerate until I've completely lost control, but the bottom arrives in the nick of time. There's a jolt of adrenalin from nearly falling and I tell myself to be more careful. It's a steep pull back up the other side calling for another set of muscles. I push on as hard as I can.

Over the top, there's a runnable stretch down through the woods back to the river. The trail twists and turns as it makes its way steeply downhill and I'm watching my footing, being careful not to go too fast, sensing pain in my thighs every time I try to brake. Stephen Cousins overtakes me as the hill levels off.

A minute or two later we're climbing again and have to slow to a walk. But his light ahead spurs me on, and I soon overtake him back. Then I'm watching for a hidden left turn and it comes quicker than expected, the Centurion sign guiding the way shines reassuringly in my headtorch beam.

Reunited with the Thames again, the path is heading upstream along the right bank. Through a gate and there's suddenly river mist - thick and icy cold, strangely inverted so I'm running with my eyeline level with its swirling base. Last year poor visibility hampered people and I fear there may be thicker stuff to come.

It's dark and eerie and there's now no-one else around. The silence is broken by the call of an owl, somewhere close. The river seems more alive, more potent than it did during the daytime. Its surface is elusive because of the mist, but I can smell its dampness and aura and they feel colder than the surrounding air.

I pass underneath a railway bridge and the echo from my footfall is amplified by the stillness. I know from my recce this is the Great Western Railway crossing the Thames for a second time and heading over to the east bank for a few miles. Here river and railway share similar chicanery as they take the line of least resistance through the hills.

It's beginning to feel properly like the middle of the night. Conscious I'm being chased, I keep the pace as high as possible. One minute I'm in a grassy meadow, the next back to compacted mud, watching out for tree roots. There's no need to think, just negotiate the undulations and stay away from the left edge where the river must be only a few inches away.

My connection to the path is much more symbiotic now than it was yesterday morning. We're going in the same direction, covering the same contours, and after fifteen hours conjoined, I'm conditioned to its mood, its camber and pitch, the amount of give in its surface (8). All are feeding back to some still awake part of my brain and helping me adjust, and where necessary alter, my speed and stride length.

Ok, so we should be seeing the glow of Streatley's lights over there above the trees sometime soon? No not for now. Jog on through another wood, try not to slow down too much. Here's the town eventually, and finally on the bridge between Goring and Streatley, Stephen Cousins is overtaking me again. At least I made him work for it!

Then, a couple of hundred metres further on, there are Centurion banners and signs asking us to be quiet as we enter Streatley aid station. The wood panelled hall is warm and welcoming and there's a sleepy vibe inside.

I've made it within the 60 minute target, got to 71 miles already, and for the last hour at least, been totally absorbed in what I'm doing. This has already become a very special experience, the high point of a lifetime of running.

2 THANKS TO RAY

It's teatime after school, I'm in the front bedroom of our house in Kingswood in Kent and sunlight is filling the south facing space. Ray, a colleague of Dad's, is redecorating, and the wallpaper filled with American trains – the backdrop to my childhood - is being systematically scraped off. My brother has gone off to university and as the youngest, the last of my brothers and sisters left at home, I'm missing him a lot and have got more time on my hands. At least there's no more A-ha on the cassette player...

Somehow, we get talking about running, and Ray has an enthusiasm for the sport that's infectious, for half marathons especially. He reels off local towns that host them, stories of races he's done. I'm intrigued by the distance. It's far enough to be challenging, not so far, it's out of reach.

Soon I'm figuring out a mile long loop of our village, and then I'm out prepping for my first race: the Faversham Half Marathon 1986.

I have earlier memories of running, cross country at Swadelands School in Lenham for example. Mr. Cox, with his crimson tracksuit and sandy moustache, sending our class of 11 year olds out onto the North Downs for our PE lesson. We cross over the A20 and are soon labouring up a long hill. At the top we follow his instructions and turn right along the ancient Pilgrims' Way (9). After ten minutes or so we make the dreaded steep left turn to grind up and around the giant cross on the side of the hill, the war memorial exposing the white bedrock and dominating the valley hereabouts.

Fighting for breath, me and Carl Spencer are on our own up at the front and soon looping round the top of the Cross – all downhill from here. Hang on a mo, what's going on now? Apparently, Mr. Cox has told everyone to double back when the leaders come past. Sorry, what?! We're joined by more worldly-wise classmates who've dodged out of the hardest bit, suddenly competing for the lead. I'm spent and stop trying, frustrated at the pointlessness of my effort…

But this time thanks to Ray's encouragement, I'm running for myself and making up the rules. There's no internet, no training manual, I've no idea what I'm doing. But I'm enthusiastic and over a few weeks build some fitness and head out for some longer runs.

Race day. Mum there to support me. Other runners milling around the start in a narrow country lane, autumnal rain in the air. After what seems like an age for everyone to unwind across the line, there's the excitement of running in a completely new place, each turn bringing a new scene change. Then disappointment at walking near the finish, a time of 1 hour 49 minutes and the desire to do it again. Other half marathons follow…

Canterbury next, a lesson in pacing. Sprinting downhill through the city centre I can see the leaders of the race. But the flaw in my strategy is all to clear when we head into hillier terrain and I have to slow up. The London Marathon winner Mike Gratton is finishing one of the race loops as I start it. His bearded face is focused as he works his way up a steep drag, peerless, out on his own.

Then it's the Hastings Half, an introduction to a more challenging course profile. Five miles in there's the dreaded

Queensway hill. We're all strung out and I'm doing my best to follow Ray's advice to focus only on the next lamppost. A few miles further on, I pair up with another runner and we make progress together for a while, but somewhere in the Old Town I lose him and slow up again. The section along the sea front takes ages in a strong headwind. I end up just over the two hour mark, holding a medal with an engraving of a Norman soldier on it.

Aylsham is the venue for my next race, an old coal mining town, a schooling in running in the heat. Everything goes ok until the last hill which is too hard in the higher temperature and I have to walk most of it. My sister Heather, home from university for the summer, is sat by the side of the road at the finish, reading a book while she waits.

And then Maidstone. I go to the Grammar here so it's my home race – an out and back 13.1 miles along the North Downs, rolling terrain. Everything comes together and I complete the distance without walking, get the coveted 1 hour 45 minutes time I've been aiming for all along.

And that could well have been that as far as my running career was concerned. Job done and onto other things. After university I became an outdoor instructor and forgot about it… Mr. Cox graded me C1 on my school report at Swadelands. Top marks for effort but decidedly average when it comes to sporting ability.

And yet, thanks to Ray, and his well-timed piece of youth work, a seed had been planted at a formative time. I hadn't set the world alight, but I'd loved running being my thing, not knowing what was round the next corner, the idea of training to go faster and further.

3 THE LONDON STONE

There are around 300 of us stood expectantly along the Thames towpath in Richmond. It's a cold but sunny spring day; unthreatening white clouds are being carried quickly across the sky on a northerly wind which also ruffles up the river. I'm about to do another race and have gained a bit more experience since those early efforts in the 1980s. In a nod to ultra running convention my race number 58, is pinned to my shorts rather than my tee-shirt.

James Elson, the Centurion race director is counting down from 10. Time seems to slow in the final moments before the start.

Around me are people with powerful stories who've been working for months if not years to get here, families and friends are watching on.

Richard quit drink and drugs a decade back and describes himself as 'hooked on running' now. Naomi fought back from a stress fracture of her leg in 2017 but then faced the disappointment of having to drop out from this race last year; she's determined to make the finish this time. Giacomo had brain surgery in 2011 to help manage his epileptic seizures – since then he's run every day.

After four 50 milers in one year, Brian is well known on

the ultra circuit, but he's never done a 100 mile race before. Neither has Ben, who wants to get a one day belt buckle first time round. Alex volunteered on the race in 2017, ran it last year and now wants to go sub 24 too. Spencer is attempting to beat the one day cut off at the fifth time of asking. His friend Helen is stood nearby doing her second 100; they may run together later.

In village halls, rowing clubs and pop up marquees up ahead, volunteers like Michelle, Lou and Ivor are giving up their weekends to mark the route, set up and staff aid stations, and do whatever it takes to support our efforts, to help keep us moving. Many won't get any sleep tonight.

There are only a few seconds to go. This moment has been coming for a long time and I want to try and enjoy it. I look left and catch my wife Ilaria's eye. She's put up with a great deal supporting me through highs and lows in the build up to this race. Now she shouts 'Come on Gazza' excitedly as ultra running legend Dan Lawson sounds the hooter and we slowly, inexorably roll forwards.

Stood next to Ilaria is Laura, who lives nearby, and has come down to support as well. As she films on her phone, race banners flutter in the breeze, Dan gives a couple more exuberant blasts of the hooter and dogs bark to join in as the pack moves off from the front with a concertina effect.

We're away and running, and it feels good. I've given myself one hour and 57 minutes to get to the first aid station at Walton, 9.45 minutes per mile.

Early on I'm trying not to over think things, soaking in the camaraderie with the other runners, and taking in the scenery – a quiet islet in the middle of the river, an eye-catching scarlet houseboat, newly unfurled leaves blowing in the breeze with a just painted look as they flash by in the sun.

I'm also scanning the trail about eight feet ahead, seeking out the softest terrain, the line with the most give and the least impact.

Around the 5k mark we get to Teddington Lock. I know somewhere here Rosemary, my CEO, will have brought her three-year-old daughter Erin down to watch the race. I see them up ahead on a bridge, and wave. They spot me and shout and take a picture. Job done. Everyone happy!

Kingston comes next and we cross over to the right bank. An hour's gone already. I'm becoming aware of the mix of personalities around me and sometimes catch their names printed below their race numbers. I'm following Nick who has a nice rhythm… chatting easily with Alex who tells me about doing the race last year… passing and then being passed by a man doing the race in sandals who's moving disconcertingly fast, when he's not breaking off to walk for a bit… then admiring the relaxed attitude of another guy in the race, carefully composing a landscape shot of the river on his phone, as we go by Hampton Court Palace.

Back on the left bank, there's a couple at a café having a leisurely Saturday morning coffee, the Moseley boathouses, Sunbury Lock. Before long we reach the aid station at 12 miles. It's 11.27 and for now I'm right on schedule.

Ilaria and her cousin are here with her three sons. It's a boost to see them and we chat briefly. Then a volunteer fills up my drinks bottles, I grab a couple of biscuits and set off again. As this is my last bit of support until Reading, I cross Walton Bridge with a little spurt, to put on a show for the audience.

A park, a wood, a lock go by, then a few miles further on, somewhere between Shepperton and Chertsey, a group of runners come past me. I'm starting to feel tired and kicking myself for getting two refills of the powdered Tailwind drink rather than water at Walton. I build in a few walking breaks for the first time.

I've trained enough over the last two years for 20 miles to seem relatively straightforward. So 15 shouldn't be this hard and I shouldn't be falling behind my timing schedule already? I can sense salty sweat on my forehead, I'm really thirsty too. My heart rate is much higher than it should be, which is concerning, and we're running north into a blustery headwind on this stretch. I'm becoming weighed down by the enormity of the challenge, all the miles ahead, worrying what the rest will be like if I'm already going through a bad patch this early on.

Ok time to give myself a pep talk, try and de-escalate this. One - accept you're dehydrated and sort it as soon as you can. Two - your high heart rate is probably due to the stress of the race or the dehydration, don't worry about it for now. Three - don't push too hard, just think about getting to the 20 mile point at Staines and walk when necessary. I use a gentle tone to help this stuff sink in (10). And it does calm me down and start to make everything more bearable

When I eventually get to Staines, the other competitors' crews are around for the first time – alert, well drilled teams, flanked by bags of food, drink, and other paraphernalia. They're not there for me but they clap all the same and at this low point, their support means a lot.

Somewhere here too is the London Stone – the last place a high tide is discernible on the Thames (11) and a sign this section of our journey, getting out of the city, is nearly done. As if to confirm it, ten minutes or so later, over on the left bank, the path passes under the M25 bridge. It's a morale boost passing this landmark after twenty-one and a half miles of running – normally I'd be zipping along overhead doing 70 in the car.

And then thankfully it's Wraysbury, the second aid station. My carefully calibrated schedule dictates a four minute stop. I might take more than that! I remember some advice from the Andy Mouncey ultra book – in a longer race, problems can become 'compound and cumulative' (12) – be proactive in diagnosing and dealing with issues early, otherwise the wheels will come off…

I climb the steps into the pavilion area determined to fix things. I have a long drink of water. An attentive volunteer fills my portable containers with water. I tuck them back in the front sleeves of my lightweight pack. I have some much-needed ham sandwiches, some crisps and some watermelon. I take some sweets. A pee in the loo confirms my urine is already becoming brown in colour and I'm dehydrated. More water, more ham sandwiches and then I sit down outside to put a blister plaster on my big toe.

I'm feeling way better when I leave. The seven minutes at Wraysbury have been the most productive and valuable of the race so far…

4 MILLENNIUM FALCON

I've got Snow Patrol going on the MP3 player as running comes into fashion in my life again.

A couple of colleagues coax me out for a jog along the Forest Way, the old railway track between East Grinstead and Groombridge. I enjoy it and get talked into doing the Reading Half Marathon. My friend Kyle bets that I'll be slower than two hours, but I sneak in under it by the skin of my teeth.

It's going to be a special year. I'm in an exciting new relationship, she's into running and we get into the habit of racing along the Forest Way together first thing on a summer morning, before everyone else is up. In a bid to impress her I sign up for the Vale of Pewsey Half Marathon in August - it goes better than Reading and I get a new PB.

Then almost as soon as it's begun the new relationship is over. I've invested a lot of hope in it and fall back to earth with a bump. Winter's coming and all the momentum has gone. I'm feeling alone and inadequate, wondering how I've become so low, if there's any way out from this despondency.

When I moved to Edinburgh to do a Master's a few years before, I'd also had some mental health difficulties -

uprooted and in a new country, not knowing anyone. I figured the five miles from my room to the campus was runnable and ran it. As well as helping get grounded in the new city, it provided some relief from how I felt.

An idea develops and when a place on the 2006 London Marathon becomes available with London Youth (13) the charity I work for, I jump at the chance. The same night, the last day of November 2005, I start training. And from that first run onwards, something hardens within me and I throw myself into the project with abandon. 25 miles the first week, 30 the second.

After a few weeks the training has a slingshot effect on my mood - the despair and rejection, all my negative feelings are being channelled in a completely new direction. Running takes my mind off things but it's also starting to take on an energy of its own.

One time I run in the dark and the wet all week. On the Sunday night, driving down to the Forest Way, horizontal sleet and snow starts to zoom towards the windscreen. There's so much white stuff flying past, it's like the Millennium Falcon as it makes the jump to light speed. I start banging the steering wheel, shouting to psyche myself up - 'IS THAT THE BEST YOU'VE GOT? BRING IT ON!'

And at the same time loosely following a training schedule, I'm running further than ever before: a 14 miler with my sister Heather following on her bike, 16, 17 miles (ice bath after that one) and then 20.

After three or four months of effort my fitness is building. Starting off is like turning the engine on in a car, I know I'm going to get a response. I decide London is doable in under 3 hours 30 minutes.

Time for some races to practise. Dover Half Marathon in the rain, a 20 mile race in Thanet. Then the Milton Keynes Half Marathon, Sunday 12th March 2005.

Walking down to the start, the London Marathon theme music blares out from two large speakers and I get goose bumps. A switch flicks in my head. Sod taking practise races easy, the focus on the marathon, I'm like a greyhound ready to be released from the traps. And this is my distance…

A hooter sounds and we're off. I let myself get pulled along towards the front of the pack and manage the first three miles in under 20 minutes. I figure 10 miles at seven minute mile pace is within my grasp. I have a breather then pick it up again, follow a club runner who seems to be going well.

The guy I'm with slows up in the headwind as we go around a lake, so it's time to overtake, tuck in behind someone else, endure the pain and keep going. I'm fighting for breath, and trying to hang on, but manage to reach 10 miles in just under 70 minutes. Satisfied for now, I slow up for a bit, but then get a second wind and push hard again on the last stretch.

At the 13 mile marker my watch says 1 hour 30 minutes and something seconds. I'm going to make it the whole way round just inside 7 minute mile pace – way faster than I thought possible. I experience a surge of euphoria unlike anything that's gone before and catch myself shouting at the sheer thrill of it. After the rejection and the long runs through the winter, here in the spring sunshine is potency. I sprint the last 100 metres or so and cross the finish line in one hour 31 minutes. Afterwards I wander around in a happy daze, demons duly battled.

Later I'll figure my goal-setting worked – the 10 mile target had been doable and after that the pressure had been taken off and I'd carried on uninhibited through to the finish.

Feeling rather invincible, I do 55 miles the next week, and 64 the week after. And then, after months of pushing it and racing hard, I get a sharp pain on the inside of my right knee and have to stop training for a few weeks. After the impetus I've built up, it is deflating. And the idea that sub

3.30 for the marathon is achievable, starts to slip away. At least after seeing the osteopath, and a lot of rest, I am able to do the race.

At the start in Greenwich Park I chat nervously to my friend Clare who's come to support me. My Mum died from breast cancer a few years before and we'd been close. I tell myself she would have been here too.

We're called out through the park gates and this time I'm aiming not to go off too fast. Early on there's a wall of noise on the long sweep round Cutty Sark.

Things quieten down, but there's still shoulder to shoulder crowds along the pavement, someone handing out orange quarters, water stations stretching on forever, staffed by local young people.

Then it's Tower Bridge - crowds everywhere, and a deafening noise. It's as if we're on a giant stage and I'm making an effort to soak everything in.

Ten minutes or so further on, helicopters overhead build excitement and the elite men flash by on the other side of the barriers, almost impossibly fast. A glimpse and they're gone.

I'm looking for my sister and Clare on the Isle of Dogs but can't see them. To make matters worse I'm now taking more than eight minutes per mile for the first time. Things start to blur by Canary Wharf. I try to follow a woman in a black tee-shirt but lose concentration, the elastic snaps and she disappears.

A voice in my head tells me to watch my bad knee. I can't seem to react as the sub 3.30 pacer group comes by. My goal is slipping away, and I can only run in slow motion. We're in a claustrophobic tunnel and I'm going slower and slower.

Back in the daylight lager-swigging supporters are yelling 'COME ON GAZZA' with a surely-you-can-go-faster-than-that urgency. But I can't, I've slowed to 10 minute miles and know only pain and confusion hereabouts. Someone's moved the mile markers much further apart.

Later, on the Embankment, a sympathetic voice in the crowd calls out "Only 3k to go Gazza. You can do this." He's a runner, he understands. Big Ben looms and the fog suddenly clears - running becomes simple again. Along Birdcage Walk then a set of signs say 800, 600, 400 metres to go as we pass Buckingham Palace. Crossing the line, my watch says 3.36.29. I've just run a marathon!

There was a lot to take away from these last 12 months. I trained for the marathon but with hindsight, felt I hadn't prepared enough for what it would feel like mentally - I'd been unsure how to respond when my goal was slipping away. Yet although I'd trained for London, the Milton Keynes race was way more powerful. Inadvertently I'd found a non-pressured method of goal setting there that worked for me, as well as the prospect of a running nirvana. I wanted more experiences like that in the future.

5 WHAT HAPPENS NEXT?

On the far side of Wraysbury aid station there's a sweeping left hand turn in the river. I'm walking round it for a few minutes to help digestion.

The Magna Carta Memorial is only 100 metres or so away (14), but I'm not doing sightseeing this afternoon, just focusing on starting to run again, finding a rhythm which will get me to 26.2 miles inside four and a half hours. No need to push too hard, 11 minute miles should do it. We're alongside a busy road for a bit in a little wooded valley, and then the route veers right, back along the river through Old Windsor.

And all the time, the Thames is there but not there, a constant, a calming influence on the edge of my awareness. I like the way runner and academic Vybarr Cregan-Reid calls this kind of attention 'soft fascination' – our brains are hard wired to be drawn to, and nourished by, the natural environment without any pressure to actively concentrate on it (15).

Past Old Windsor Lock, our flow is interrupted by the steep steps up on to Albert Bridge. I've been in the vicinity of another competitor called Nick for hours and we chat for a minute while we're crossing over the bridge. He's friendly

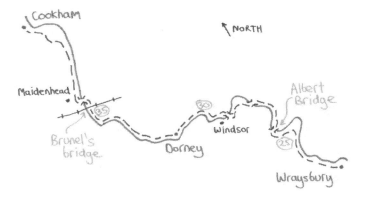

and gives me advice on the walk-run strategy he's been using.

We get to marathon distance in 4 hours 28 minutes on a little detour away from river. Here on the narrow single-track path, hemmed in by a field of crops, there's a resigned, authoritative bellow of 'there's more of them' from up ahead and we meet some harassed looking ramblers stood aside to let us pass, 'afternoon, thank you, thanks a lot…'

Moving along the pavement in Datchet I notice a very dark cloud for the first time over to our right. It's clearly about to chuck it down. That didn't show up on the BBC Weather app!

We're approaching Windsor, we've crossed Albert Bridge, and Victoria Bridge must undoubtedly follow. Over the bridge, running past a marquee in the park, the heavens open and I stop to put my lightweight waterproof on, irritated at even more time lost from the schedule. The downpour is only brief, ending as abruptly as it started, but there's another stop to put the jacket away, it's too hot running otherwise.

Into Windsor town centre, past the crews again, warmly encouraging us, past the 28 mile mark by the railway station where my first recce stopped, then there's a guy in a Centurion tee-shirt at the main town bridge directing us where to go.

Soon I'm jogging gently across a meadow in the sun, the rain a distant memory, under the other Windsor train line curving north to Slough; then on past a road bridge to more meadows, the next aid station somewhere up ahead. I'm tired again and can't think right now…

When it comes, Dorney aid station is a welcome sight. I jog in across the timing mat just a few seconds before 3pm. Five and a half hours down, 50k in the legs.

There's a small marquee on the river bank, some on-it volunteers, runners milling around. I fill my disposable cup with water for the first time. It's the one I take with me on my Southern Rail commute and I take a thirsty slug. Hmmm could have rinsed that out a bit better, that's decidedly coffee flavoured water. Let's be really really careful not to vomit here.

I recognise Helen from the #TP100 stuff on Twitter, she's cut her lip in a fall. A volunteer is listening and looking with concern, but she doesn't seem bothered and gives off a distinct tough-as-boots vibe. Another guy nearby looks much wearier, and announces he's dropping from the race. He wants to know how to get a lift home. Other runners visibly flinch at this, let's not get pulled down that line of thought…

Speaking of which, my longest training runs this year have been no further than 30 miles. Normally I'd be stopping and heading off for a bath about now. But today (and tomorrow) there are still 70 miles to go. While having something to eat, I work out I'm already 15 minutes behind my sub 24 hour schedule. This is not going to be like London, where falling behind threw me. In my head I decide to tear the schedule into little pieces, and immediately feel better. The only way to face the distance ahead is to give myself plenty of time and concentrate on a finish within 28 hours. Forget about the one day belt buckle.

A weight is lifted. Liberated, I set off along the river towards Maidenhead at a relaxed walk. The scenery is sublime, the sun flickering through the new leaves, yellow celandines in the grass and May blossom scattered everywhere. The trail weaves in and out of the trees, leading invitingly into the middle distance. The mud is soft and compacted, the surface flat and, dare I say it, runnable. What was Nick saying to me on Albert Bridge? What if I did eight minutes running and two walking? That might be doable. That might be a plan.

The first eight minutes of running are wonderful and uninhibited. So good I don't want to stop when they're done. No, stick to the new strategy and make the most of the two minute breather. Eight minutes on, two minutes off. Let the woods and meadows roll by; let the GPS watch keep itself busy and repeatedly show 11 minutes something seconds as it vibrates at the end of each digital mile.

Into Maidenhead and we're coming up to Brunel's red brick railway bridge over the river. The one I noticed on the recce a few weeks back - the centrepiece of 19th century modernity that moved Turner so much he made it the subject of the ephemeral 'Rain, Steam and Speed' (16). I'm annoyed to notice some graffiti across the stonework, surely that wasn't there last time?

It's about ten to four as we cross the main bridge in Maidenhead, over onto the left hand bank. Even though the little hill up onto the bridge has eased off, other competitors around me are still walking. I start running again to overtake them. The little spurt down the bridge into Berkshire turns into a longer one and there's a grin on my face at still wanting to race in mile 36. I'm in the middle of the field but that's ok. This is fun! A chance to distract lumbering mind and body.

An ominous looking cloud appears again and there's another shower just before Boulter's Lock. There's a pitstop to put the jacket on but then I push myself to carry on running through the heavy rain. Past the crews again, boosted by the clapping, I overtake a few more people and convince myself I'm leading a little pack. I veer right, soon back by the river jogging through woods on the way to Cookham.

It's not raining anymore and getting hot again. Without thinking I stop, and in a few seconds stuff the jacket away, get the pack back on and start going again, surrounded by a little race bubble, absorbed, enjoying myself.

Overhanging trees are turning the Thames emerald in colour, and the scenery feels wilder than before. Then the path gets to the end of the little gorge and turns left away from the river. A few minutes later we zigzag through an alleyway and end up in the centre of Cookham. Follow the acorn marker posts along the main road, jog through a photogenic, flowery churchyard and then back out on the riverside, in the first meadow out of town, are the tell-tale Centurion banners and a pop-up marquee.

Arriving at the Cookham aid station, I'm struck by the unfolding, random nature of the race. Yes, the training has been important, and so has checking out the route and doing mental preparation. But these things only go so far.

The last few hours have been heavily influenced by unplanned events - the chance conversation with Nick on the bridge, the unexpected rain, the cut and thrust of racing other competitors.

In The Happiness Dictionary Dr Tim Lomas links this theme to the Sanskrit word 'Anātman', which relates to all existence being reliant on 'the shifting play of circumstance.' We are all 'a dynamic, kaleidoscopic product of our encounters with other people, situations, events, the whole world around us' (17).

I often fall into the trap of being closed and anxious in new situations. But for this one day by the Thames, I am not going to feel like that. The race has a compelling, seize-the-day unpredictability and I will continue to have no idea what happens next. For once I allow myself to see just how beautiful and exciting that could be.

6 AN ODYSSEAN EDUCATION

After London my appetite for running was satisfied for a time and my life moved on. I met Ilaria in November that year and we got married a few years later. She showed me the merits of Mediterranean holidays and our summers together in Italy and Greece became the highlight of my year. And my career changed – I became a professional fundraiser with London Youth. Through a long period of austerity, my charity's mission – out of school opportunities for young Londoners who wouldn't otherwise have access to them - felt crucial and I was totally absorbed in my work.

After some abortive attempts at reigniting my running, a niggly Achilles injury and a failed attempt to do London again ten years later, I eventually got training seriously once more in the winter of 2016-17, in preparation for the Manchester Marathon.

Browsing the running section of a bookshop in Brighton, looking for inspiration, I randomly picked up Dean Karnazes' book 'Ultramarathon Man.' I was hooked from page one - he's running through the night and getting hungry, so he calls up a takeaway company and asks them to meet him with a pizza a bit further down the road (18). Early on in his first 100 mile race, the Western States across

California, he describes struggling up a very steep climb for the first four miles. Up on the top someone says to him 'see that hill about 20 miles over there, the finish is 75 miles beyond that!' For me it wasn't just the seemingly impossible nature of the ultras he was doing – intriguing as they were - it was the journeying aspect, how you get to see the world differently when you travel under your own steam. The story of Odysseus captivated me when I was nine years old; the pull towards journeying seems hard-wired into all of us; and journeys had provided some of the most formative experiences of my life, given me more of a schooling for ultra running than I might have realised…

A teenage journey taught me to keep going…

My brother Ian and I spent three summers in a row travelling around the Lake District on foot. We got up there on the National Express night bus, then youth hostelled, stuffing everything we needed for the fortnight into those boxy 80s rucksacks Karrimor did. His was blue, mine was green. Something like 'Drive' by The Cars or Elton John's 'Nikita' was playing on the pub juke boxes. Maybe a bit of Madonna as well.

One day we decide to walk across the whole county – tabbing it from Patterdale to Eskdale for as long as it takes. Getting up at half four in the morning, we scramble up and over Helvellyn where, being a bit older, he makes me have a jam sandwich in the stony summit shelter. Down the other side we're caught in torrential rain which, in typical Cumbrian fashion, sets in for the day. We then get helplessly lost up on the next hill. Eventually locating the right track, we descend out of the worst of the weather. I nearly flood the outside toilet at a National Trust café emptying rainwater from my boots. And treating it like an aid station before knowing they existed, we have five cups of coffee and four of tea - you got a big pot in those days!

We continue down Borrowdale then up a never-ending

climb to Esk Hause, where we're nearly lifted off our feet during a squally shower. Down the other side and running out of gas we plough unthinkingly through a bog, sinking up to our knees in the quagmire. Finally, about six o'clock there's a small patch of blue sky and a short while later the sun comes out. That evening we stagger down to the local pub in Eskdale for Cumberland Sausage and Chips. We've managed our crossing of the whole district in one of the worst days of the summer. We talk about 'the 35 mile walk' in reverent tones for years to come.

Another experience a year or so later showed me what happens when you step outside your comfort zone…

Taking 12 months out before university I save all year for an organised trek to K2. Having spent my boyhood soaking up mountaineering books I am drawn to Concordia, an area of Northern Pakistan where there's a cluster of remote and very high mountains. It's June 1988, and I've never travelled beyond France before, so the first day in Rawalpindi is overwhelming: 46 degrees, 100 per cent humidity, crowded streets saturated with colour and Arabic script, an intimidating level of noise and traffic.

Then we hear flights to Skardu are grounded and we need to commandeer a bus up the Karakoram Highway instead. These are a long 24 hours. They start out alright. On the Grand Trunk Road out of Islamabad someone slides a Joshua Tree tape in the music player. As the familiar opening chords of 'Where the streets have no name' fill the bus, everything feels better and I'm suddenly carefree and excited, aware anything could happen.

The day gets hotter and the road gets rougher. We spend hundreds of kilometres following the Indus River, coloured grey by the surrounding rock and glacier melt. We stop for lunch in a dusty wild west kind of town.

Later, well into the afternoon, the trip cameraman, sat in the row of seats in front of me, becomes unwell and without any warning vomits out of the window. The bus is open-sided, and the wind splatters it back in the bus and over my arms and legs. There's nowhere to get cleaned up.

Afternoon becomes evening. Through the hours of darkness I can see a red, presumably drug-induced, glow in the driver's eyes and don't feel comfortable going to sleep as we wobble along the precarious rubbly road, the turbulence of the river hundreds of feet below.

The trek begins, and in the mountains, I'm more at home. There's a distinctive earthy smell here which is completely new but not unpleasant. We adjust to the temperature swings of the Karakoram, swapping Factor 50 during the day for down jackets when the sun sets.

At the end of the first week we climb up onto the Baltoro Glacier. Stark and striking peaks from mountaineering folklore are visible left and right - the Trango Towers, Mustagh Tower, Masherbrum, Gasherbrum, Broad Peak, distant avalanches too.

And then after four days scrambling across ice and rock up the Baltoro, down a side valley to the left, comes the impossibly beautiful, perfectly pyramidal hill we've come to see. K2 is silent and hypnotic and strangely emotional. For someone who previously had Helvellyn as their reference point for a mountain, its scale, its imperious vertical wall of snow and ice, is hard to take in.

A few of us are drawn further up the glacier and spend a night at K2 Base Camp. The jump-suited multi-national mountaineers are lean and exotic, with a glint in their eye as if they've found what they're looking for.

It's a long trek back the way we've come, and our diet of dehydrated food starts to feel oppressive. I'm homesick and yearn for fish and chips. By Askole we're nearly done, and with blissful ignorance of the risks, I buy some of the local eggs and our Balti cook fries them for me. After weeks of powdered vegetable curry, the fattier food tastes heavenly. But my stomach is soon rumbling ominously and I'm in for a troubled night.

The next morning the schedule for the last day is to do a tough, long push through the Braldu Gorge. Although I've been sick six or seven times and that's not showing any signs of stopping, there's no option for me to stay behind otherwise I'll miss the flight home. My Balti friend Ghulam Ali is my saviour that day. We've always enjoyed our 'Salaam Alaikum – Alaikum Salaam' exchanges and similar sense of humour. Now he stays by my side for the long hours through the gorge, coaxing me up all the shaly climbs and covering my back on the descents. A watching ultra runner might have noted me gritting my teeth and grinding it out to get through this. I'd rather associate that day with Ghulam Ali's help – something for which I'll always be grateful.

And finally, a more pastoral experience in 2014, offered a glimpse of the spiritual benefits of journeying. I walked down Wales with Ace, a friend since our time as outdoor instructors together in our early twenties.

We pose for a picture on the beach in Prestatyn and then, carrying everything we need for the journey, follow Offa's Dyke Path south towards Llangollen. In the first few days over the Clwydian Hills my job stays near the top of my mind. But after a while, being outside all day, experiencing unspooling countryside at two miles an hour starts to have an impact. We see a lamb being born, a stoat scampering away, a red kite close up. I'd never heard of the Vale of Clwyd before now and it takes three days to walk past it. There's a special moment as some of my colleagues and Paul's family accompany us for a day.

Then on the seventh day we pull over the top of Hawthorn Hill and without warning, for the first time in ages, there's a completely new view to the south. An uninterrupted sweep of rolling hills and unpeopled valleys for mile after mile. It's not just that it's beautiful and humbling to suddenly see the southern half of Wales spread out before us, it's that we've worked hard to get it. The view feels like a reward and a sense of well-being stays with us as we carry on for four more days towards the sea. Reaching the Severn Estuary is poignant. It's rewarding to have walked the length of Wales, but I want to keep going.

In the spring of 2017, finishing the Dean Karnazes book, I decide there and then I'm going to do a 100 mile race – to combine running and journeying. I sign up for a 50k and a 50 miler later that year. I read more ultra books, trawl the internet for YouTube videos about the Western States and other races, and I start learning about the mental side of ultras. This helps when I finally get to the Manchester Marathon. With Ilaria there in support, I unexpectedly shave a minute off my PB and roll home pleased with myself in 3 hours 35 minutes.

7 A DIFFERENT WORLD

Setting off along Cookham Reach, everything ahead of me is mellow – an easy-going river, a meadow made luminous by the recent rain, and for now at least, an innocent-looking, cobalt blue sky. I'm ready for the unexpected. I have my eight minutes running, two minutes walking strategy. Eating, drinking and being business-like at the aid station felt like the right thing to do, but now I'm off again, captivated by the scene in front of me and ready to enter back into the race arena.

Since giving up on the timing schedule I've felt less pressure, and this is freeing me up to push harder. Somewhere below the surface, my dream of finishing in a single day is still intact.

Half a mile or so beyond the checkpoint comes the bridge at Bourne End. I turn left and climb the steep steps. A set of previously resting muscles are woken up and quite understandably irritable about it. Then I'm crossing the narrow, slightly bouncy walkway by the railway track and dropping down the far side into Buckinghamshire. There's a chocolate box, too-good-to-be-true simplicity to some of the scenery just now - it was no surprise to learn Enid Blyton

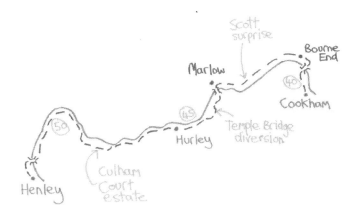

lived near here (19).

Out beyond Bourne End, the river's finished meandering round to the left and we're heading west for the next 30 miles or so. It feels wonderful chugging across pancake-flat meadows through the little valley on the way to Marlow, and I get into the groove again, marking time, establishing a 12 minute mile pace, pleasantly distracted by a little sprinter train going by in the other direction. I become aware of a female runner with a similar tempo, and we smile and hold the gates open, as our patterns of running and walking, mean we're repeatedly leap-frogging past one another.

Midway through mile 43, there's a friendly cry of 'HULLO MATE' from up ahead and Scott, ex instructor from Hindleap, is stood there, filming me on his phone, ready to hand me Skittles and water. It's a complete surprise and a thoughtful gesture, which is why I've got a big smile on my face in his film. In low moments I've thought of the little GPS device in the pocket of my pack, beaming my progress to my brothers and sisters and colleagues, hoping they might be watching dot number 58. Here's some evidence people are interested, and it spurs me on.

The Temple Bridge diversion is still in place, so we have

to cross the main bridge in Marlow town centre back onto the other bank. I know all about the diversion. I did three miles on the wrong side of the river on my recce because of missing the signs. Not this time son!

Through the other side of Bisham, the sky is no longer cobalt blue and there's another short-lived downpour, another jacket-on-jacket-off job. The last stretch of the diversion back to the river takes an age and my patience starts wearing thin. It's ok running 'aid station to aid station' as you're always told, as long as the aid station is actually there! My watch finally reads 45.6 miles rather than 44 miles when I finally get there.

Ok so another pep talk needed. This grumpiness is helping no-one – concentrate on getting more water, eating a cocktail sausage or two, hoovering some water melon and thanking the volunteers, who are as always somehow magically tuned into my wavelength. Then move slowly away from the aid station for a few minutes to digest everything, then get on with it.

There's still a lot of other runners in the vicinity and we've all been going long enough to find a sustainable way to carry on moving. It's nine hours since we started, more like evening than afternoon now; rays from the low angled sun are flickering in and out of my eyes, turning everything amber and over exposed.

On the pull up towards a big country house there's an exchange with a friendly fellow competitor. I share how frustrated I was about the mileage on the approach to Hurley. He gently suggests this is a rooky mistake - not a helpful mindset.

We climb about 100 feet above the river, the route cutting through the heart of Culham Court Estate. The evening light is warm, turning everything honey coloured. The Estate has its own chapel, made from cream coloured stone – an eye-catching silhouette to the left. Down to our right there's a manicured, private looking cricket pitch and beyond that sweeping views north across the Thames to the

Hambleden Valley and the start of the Chiltern Hills. It's as if this pastoral landscape hasn't changed much in centuries.

Speaking of which, journeying up river on foot, finding our way along its often winding course, is feeling like a throwback to simpler times, when the world was a little less known, when following a natural feature to travel up country was commonplace.

Markers appear encouraging people like me to carry on passing through and off the Estate. There's another scene change and a drop in the temperature as we roll down a subterranean country lane, completely enclosed in a dark tunnel of trees, then at the bottom, a sudden dazzle of sunlight again and The Flowerpot Inn. There's a moment to take in red bricks, colourful window boxes and a medley of expensive motorcars. Archetypal home counties England, the sort of place David Cameron might have taken a visiting head of state for Sunday lunch and a photogenic pint of pale ale.

I draw level with a paused, professional-looking, female runner and remembering the recce, confirm 'it's down to the right.' She heads off in front of me.

We're soon back on the left bank of the river and heading past Hambleden Lock - the beginning of a sweeping left-hand turn. My watch vibrates to say we're at 50 miles – a supposedly significant number, but I don't want to think too hard about – it might make me more aware of how much energy has gone already.

Our running and walking intervals mean I'm passing, and being passed by, competitors on the last couple of miles into Henley. I recognise Helen again and this time she's teamed up with her friend Spencer – the man with the spectacular sunglasses and witty GIFs – still going for his one day belt buckle. We draw level with the regatta course, and the church tower in Henley creeps slowly closer. On the far bank there's a marquee, the evening out buzz of a hundred or so well dressed guests tucking into a banquet, speeches still to come. On our side there are boathouses with sloping forecourts; three tall well-spoken youths come past in the opposite direction.

Finally, we're in the town centre and the path veers round to the left through a narrow walled section. There's a sudden flash of high fashion as I nearly collide with a group heading off for a night out. It's been a couple of hours since Marlow and I walk across the bridge into Oxfordshire doing my best to comprehend the sudden hubbub of civilisation.

I turn left onto a congested riverside lane and there are cars coming the other way; BMWs and Audis heading for important evening engagements. I run along the double yellow lines for a bit before I can hop across onto the towpath. It's a few more minutes along the bank before I see the Centurion banners and the aid station 100 metres or so up ahead in the meadow. This is finally half way.

But I can't stop thinking about the pub I just passed on the corner of the bridge - punters all spilled out across the pavement, savouring a Saturday night pint in the sun – close enough to see the condensation on their glasses, but they might as well have been in a different world. It's hard to explain, but for now at least I wouldn't swap places for anything. I've been moving through the landscape for so long that the normal daily patterns, the rituals and distractions, have gone and the journey has become an end in itself, keeping going is all that matters…

8 ALAN JOHN PRICE

About a fortnight after the Manchester Marathon, in April 2017, I join my 81-year-old Dad for a long weekend in Snowdonia. It's been an Easter ritual for us for nearly 10 years - staying in a hotel and walking and eating together.

Now Dad's pranged his car on a wall on the drive across from Norfolk and is unusually sheepish about it. He also reveals a mysterious iron deficiency means he's becoming breathless after about 100 metres walking; he's getting this checked out.

As he's got older Dad's become increasingly generous about letting me go off by myself in the mountains and he helps get me ready as I attempt a hair-brained scheme to run up and down Snowdon. I've got the 50k Weald Challenge race across the Ashdown Forest booked in at the end of May and it has a few more hills than Manchester. Attempting this on Easter Saturday proves a foolish idea though as there's about ten thousand people doing the Llanberis Path and not much room. I become nostalgic for the day together a few Easters before when in his late 70s, Dad made it up the mountain himself and got close to a rolling round of applause from everyone in the vicinity for the duration of his effort.

A day or two later, tradition dictates we have a trip on the Ffestiniog Railway together and he tells me - 'don't get to obsessed with this running business Gruff' - before we go our separate ways.

Training for the 50k continues back at home. I start properly trail running for the first time – exploring the off-the-beaten-track Wealdway and Vanguard Way which the race will follow; finding out a mile or two out of Uckfield, the Wealdway goes through an unspoilt river valley I never knew was there before.

Asking about 'finding that elusive run forever rhythm' on the Strava app I get some great advice from a guy called Alan Routledge about focusing on heart rate rather than speed. Keep your heart rate below 75% of maximum he tells me – mid 140s – and it's easier to go further. I've never been a technically minded runner, preferring to make things up as I go along, but I'm still following Alan's helpful advice two years on. It's an excuse to run much slower basically!

I buy a lightweight ultra pack to start taking food with me; experiment with eating enough to run sustainably, but not so much to slow me down. Longer runs, are starting to feel much more relaxed than when marathon training. In Manchester I was pounding the streets for hours with a heart rate in the 160s. Now I'm moving much slower and walking when necessary.

I read Andy Mouncey's 'So you want to run an Ultra' (20) book. It's almost deliberately unstructured – like he knows something about how organically ultras unfold. There's advice about the mental side of running, how to eat properly, how to anticipate some of the things that can go wrong; and there are stories and guidance from people who've done longer endurance races successfully. I'm surprised to see there aren't any training schedules, but this also seem refreshing. I've found marathon training schedules increasingly oppressive – the stepped progression for long runs, the prescriptive distances per week, being told when to do to tempo and when to do threshold running.

This book is a breath of fresh air in comparison.

I do my first ultra, the Weald Challenge 50k at the end of May and learn a lot.

Deciding to show off my Snowdon acquired uphill technique I run the 600 foot climb up on to the Ashdown Forest when everyone else is walking. On reaching the top I understand why. The temperature is in the 20s, my heart rate is in the mid-180s and I'm like a car radiator with smoke coming out of it. All the people I overtook come smoothly back past me doing their level best not to gloat.

At the 18 mile checkpoint I adopt an in-and-out-fast approach – fill both water bottles, hoover a slice of water melon and shoot off – the manoeuvre has moved me up about six places and I'm congratulating myself on my racing prowess, when I slow to negotiate a stile. As I lift my right leg over the top, its seized by a violent, immobilising cramp. Doubled over in agony, and barely able to move, I try to appear casual, as about six people come back past. One of them is in a helpful frame of mind – 'you need some salt mate'. Time to follow his advice and dig out the Ritz crackers.

It's great being able to jog some stretches out past marathon distance but also a bit like being one of those cartoon characters that's still running out past the end of a cliff. Any second now my body is going to figure out how long I've been going and give up. I miss out on an opportunity to finish under six hours by 20 seconds.

But there's also a real sense of accomplishment and after only one race, I'm hooked on ultras already. My mind and soul have been taken to new places and I want more. And the combination of running and journeying is energising - much of the race has been through undiscovered parts of Sussex - wild woods and old drovers' roads - long sections through the middle of nowhere which are enlightening, which fill in unchartered tracts on my map of the Weald.

It was not a problem-free experience however. My old

marathon knee injury flared up before and during the race. Realising this as a sign that three big races in one summer is too much, I pull out of my planned 50 mile race, and take some time off from running to give my knee a chance to recover.

The enforced break enables me to support Dad better as we get the news that he has bowel cancer. He develops complications after the operation to remove the tumour and has to stay in hospital longer than planned, which he hates. Me and my siblings set up a WhatsApp group and plan when we'll provide cover. I stay in Norfolk to be with him for a few weeks during August, working from his house near Aylsham and taking the train down from Norwich to London for meetings.

In September, Dad is nowhere near well enough to take charge of the walking holiday he's been planning on the Isle of Man. I deputise on his behalf and go back to the island for the first time since 1975 to hang out with his Rotarian and Norfolk Walking Group friends. He's done a great job planning four outings with geographical and historical interest and it's bitter sweet leading the journeys on his behalf. It's obvious how he's held in high regard by his friends and that his presence is sorely missed.

By October, Dad seems to have stabilised a bit and is back at home with some carer support. My knee feels better, and I start doing some gentle running. Come December I'm up to 15 miles again and ready to renew my passion for ultras. Learning from over ambition in the summer I target one race only for 2018 – the Westcountry Flat 50 Miler. Albion Running's description of the route is straight-talking (21) – start at Taunton, run 25 miles along a canal, then a river to the sea, then turn left and follow the coast path for another 25 miles to Minehead.

Dad's still giving me, and my brother and sisters concern though. Ilaria and I stay with him at Christmas and he's clearly not happy, not himself and not properly recovered. He's busy composing a strongly worded email to his Doctor proposing a revised plan of action.

Then one Monday morning in early January about ten to nine, I'm walking across London to work when my phone starts to vibrate. It's Stuart his carer calling - Dad's been vomiting and is being blue-lighted back into hospital. Through force of habit I carry on working, but the messages get worse during the morning and it's obvious I need to be up there. The train from Liverpool Street would be the quickest way, but thinking I'll be in Norfolk for a bit, I make a decision I'll always regret, and travel home to Sussex first so I can get my car and move around more easily.

I arrive at the Norfolk and Norwich Hospital just after 5pm but I'm too late. My brother Ian is there looking shell-shocked in the toilets. He won't tell me the news until we're in a private room together, but I know that the worst has happened. He confirms it, and later I go into see Dad's body with my sister Louise.

The next morning I'm running blindly along a pavementless dual carriageway on the outskirts of Norwich, horns blaring at me in the morning rush hour, trying to get the image of the pained expression on Dad's face out of my head, the only way I know how…

After the funeral and the immediate paperwork are sorted, there's a starkness to my running through the rest of that winter – a desire to go out further and further, to find a way to cauterise the grief. My mileage goes up through 30, 40, 50, 60 miles a week. I start running 11 miles into work at Hindleap Warren as the sun comes up, and 11 miles home as it goes down.

A few months later after a day disposing of Dad's belongings, I run into the North Norfolk countryside, heading off into the middle of nowhere in a cold rain, resigned to getting wet. An hour or so later after barely seeing a soul, the clouds part and as I look across the big open skies to the left, the sun comes bursting through, the temperature lifts and steam starts to rise from the glistening road surface. I'm not just running away now, I'm finding somewhere new.

By the end of April, I've done 1,000 miles in six months and after my friend Peter painstakingly and selflessly organises a set of race maps for me, I'm ready for the 50 mile race in Somerset.

It's Saturday 19th May 2018, about quarter past four in the afternoon, and running along the coast between Blue Anchor and Minehead, I still have Jaffa Cake crumbs round my face from the Dunster Beach aid station. The turf beneath my feet is short and spongy and has a pleasant give to it as each stride makes contact. The day is very warm but there's a heavenly cooling breeze blowing straight into my face. To my right the sea is calm. On my left a row of retirement chalets, an old gent reading a paper looking up as I pass, a surprised look on his face. Running still feels easy and free, easier and freer than it should do. I can't believe I've been going since half seven this morning and I'm on mile 49.

In the next 20 minutes or so I'll walk-run round Minehead Golf Club, reach the 50 mile mark, negotiate a pair of unexpected sand dunes, be chuffed and surprised by my friends Nic and Rach greeting me at the roadhead, and, seeing their smiles and support, jog on a wave of adrenalin which will carry me the mile or so to the finish. Ultras are never the exact distance advertised – this time we're getting a bonus 1.7 miles!

It's been an extraordinary day. The first two hours – tapping out nine minute miles along the Taunton and Bridgwater canal – were some of the most sublime running I've ever experienced. After the grief of the winter, it felt like a journey through the light, the chance to soak in countryside on the cusp of spring and summer, cow parsley and birdsong and a cornflower blue sky the backdrop. And in a display of sibling solidarity that's become increasingly common over the last few months, my sister Louise, and her husband Jon, joined me for a few miles on the way into Bridgwater.

There were difficult moments of course. It was slow going through the fields of long grass on the, at times pot-holed, River Parrett trail. I struggled to navigate around the noisy, dusty, strangely people-less, building site of Hinckley Point C, and enjoyed getting away from that. The steep grind into the Quantocks slowed me up. And down the other side, I got geographically challenged for five minutes or so by an everything-looks-the-same maze of avenues in a Williton housing estate.

As with the Milton Keynes race, some careful goal setting helped me out. I aimed for 10 hours overall - 25 miles in four hours, 30 miles in five hours and then ease off, allowing myself the 'luxury' of 15 minute miles or so for the last 20 miles.

The 25 and 30 mile targets worked well but I realised once I'd got to the coast and passed another runner, that there were more people behind me than in front, and that I was ahead of schedule. And that 15 minute miles would let me off the hook. Passing another three runners on the rolling coastal trail between Lilstock and Kilve got my competitive juices going.

So I didn't let up and a couple of hours later was surprised to see the girl in the lime green singlet – who I'd been running with along the River Parrett – catch me up on Watchet Hill. We ran together for a while - she thought she was 'first lady' and that we were near the front of the field. She pressed on and I thought she deserved to be ahead of me. So I felt guilty passing her on the crest of my adrenalin surge just before the finish. But I was also conscious that this was a small scale race, and I might be on for a first ever top ten finish - such an opportunity might never come along again. Recovering on the grass at the finish, I asked Dave Urwin, the race organiser for my position. I couldn't believe it when he said fourth.

The feelings from the last few miles of the race stayed

with me for weeks. Happiness and elation but also something more. A sense of wonder and amazement from staying in the zone for so long – pushing myself hard for over nine hours. Why had this felt so good?

In 'Footnotes, How Running Makes Us Human,' Vybarr Cregan-Reid talks about how easy it is to get distracted in the 21st century digital world, how tiring it is for the brain to be constantly pulled from task to task. Nowadays, we rarely get the chance to do a long and uninterrupted task where we can stay in the moment - 'without long breaths of silence, we lose sustained access to ourselves; we risk forgetting what it is like to be alive in this shard of time flanked by eternity' (22). Alongside the endorphins, the excitement and competition of the race, and the stimulation from exploring and finding the route, had been this time away from distraction, an extended period of freedom and focused mindfulness. And it had been so intense I wanted more, was sure that from now on, my running would be about seeking out similar experiences.

The 50 mile race had been one of the most potent days of my life. A chance to understand more about what I was capable of. It had taken the pain of Dad's death for me to grasp how brief life is and to bake in the mindset that it is worth properly going for it, giving it everything, endeavouring to 'honour the race', as had I told myself every time I felt like walking. I had spectacularly failed to follow Dad's advice, but at least I'd learnt something important from this period.

9 A SLICE OF SOREEN

It's about twenty to eight in the evening as I step over the 51 mile timing mat at Henley aid station.

The little marquee and tent are being supervised by a group of busy volunteers. The transition from moving to not moving is confusing. I do a few unthinking zig zags across other people's personal space before flopping down in a camping chair figuring out what to do next. Six or seven other competitors are sat around nearby. We've all had an intense day, there's friendly eye contact but not much said.

For the first time in over 10 hours I check my phone – its full of supportive messages from friends and family, people from work. It's lovely to know they're thinking about me and willing me on, but now is not the time for getting drawn back into the digital world; I need food, to change into warmer clothes.

A lady hemmed in behind the stove, who's already had over a hundred mouths to feed, passes me a bowl of pasta. It tastes amazing. Like she put her love into it. It's just what I need at exactly the right time. Sometimes saying thank you for all this care and support doesn't feel enough…

Then it's time to get my dropbag, change my top and move behind the tent to put on my warm bamboo running

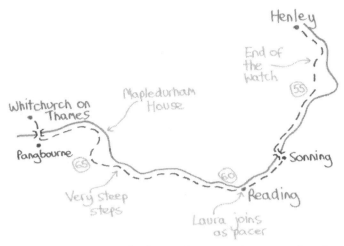

leggings. I'm not ready for such a complex procedure but manage it in the end somehow. Fifteen minutes have gone by really quickly and it's time to set off again. Leave it too long, and the magnitude of what's left to do might sink in.

Back out on the towpath I'm daunted by the thought of the next 50 miles through the night and treat myself to a quick phone call to Ilaria, already in Oxford. I tell her I'm ok and not to worry if dot number 58 slows down a lot. She's pleased to hear from me and tells me she'll see me in the morning.

The first half mile out of Henley is slow. I'm trying to use the lightweight walking poles I got from my drop bag. But it's soon clear they're going to be a hindrance rather than a help and I decide to find a way to be rid of them as soon as possible. They won't fit in my pack, so holding one folded pole in each hand, I start some gentle running across a meadow.

But getting going again, passing the spot where a Swiss banker has built a model railway for rides round the garden of his riverside house, the low battery alert vibrates on my GPS watch. Although it's inevitable I'm still a bit surprised, I've never run far enough for the batteries on my Garmin to fail before. Bugger, I thought I'd finished sorting out admin issues like this at the aid station.

None of us are perfect, I guess. Despite my new interest in ultras and mindfulness from the 50 mile race, I'm still dependent on my GPS watch for checking how far I've gone, how fast I'm running. I'm hooked on its data, don't think I can do without it. I slow to get the lead and portable charger out and set off again with the charger and watch in one hand, poles in the other. But it's impossible to see if the power is getting through from the display. All this faffing is killing my momentum - I turn the watch off and stop and put it away in my pack.

Disconnecting from this final lifeline to the digital world initially seems sacrilege but within a minute or two it's liberating. I tell myself I'm Luke Skywalker turning off his tracking computer! From now on in I'll be relying on my basic 80s Casio watch and using the force to work out how fast I'm going.

Between here and Sonning the birdsong is getting louder, and the sun is fighting a losing battle with the horizon. There's still enough light to see for longer than you'd think but passing through a darker wooded section I worry about tripping over exposed tree roots in the path and stop and dig out my headtorch.

A group of three runners have stopped to sort out their gear immediately after the road bridge at Sonning, then there's Giacomo, Mr. 'Six-Year-Run-Streak' himself, I recognise his lime green compression socks from our chat at the start. We leap frog each other for a bit, too focused on shutting out the pain to talk.

There's a lot of light still visible in the western sky along here. I start thinking how much of a boost it will be to see my friends Clare and Laura at 58 miles. The last part across a meadow goes quickly and before long the lights of Reading aid station are up ahead.

Clare is there smiling at the bottom of the steps. And Laura as well. Clare has been my friend since bringing her year group to my outdoor centre in Shropshire in the early 1990s. This is the first time she's supported me on a race since London in 2006 and it's great to see her.

It's nearly 10 o'clock on a Saturday night but my friend Laura from work is excited too – she's a talented runner, passionate about the sport, and selflessly here to be my official pacer over the next 9 miles to Whitchurch, despite the fact it's less than two weeks since she set a PB in the London Marathon. (We're allowed this support at any point from 51 miles onwards; transport logistics mean this is the best leg for her to do.)

We go up some steep steps at the side of the Wokingham Waterside Centre and into the warm indoor area on the first floor. Seven aid stations into the race, there's yet another volunteer offering to fill my water bottles – tuned in to each runner despite doing it dozens of times already. Then there's an opportunity to scoff some sausage rolls and crisps while Laura takes some photos, to smile and say I can't believe how well it's going.

Just wanting bite sized bits of food, I turn down the generously sized fruitcake I asked Clare to make for me. She's known me long enough not to mind. Or at least I hope that's the case! It's noticeably colder when we go outside again, and I give Clare a hug and then me and Laura set off.

Laura is understanding about the strategy of walking out of aid stations to help digestion. It's lovely to have company for the first time. She is also nice enough to take my poles off me and carry them as they won't fit in my pack. She's got her car parked at the station at Pangbourne and will take them home with her. We're soon crossing the little footbridge over the River Kennet and striding past Caversham Lock into Reading Town Centre - people on a Saturday night out coming past in the opposite direction.

The group of three comes by again and I later figure one of them is Richard – hooked on running and on his way to a spectacular 22 hour finish. Quite a few other competitors have now overtaken us as well and remembering I'm actually in a race, decide some running is overdue. Counting on every fourth step, with Laura effortless alongside, I keep jogging along up to a count of 100.

I'm increasingly sleepy and sluggish. My body clock – always regimented – associates this hour with pillow and duvets and lying down - getting ready for and going to sleep. After pushing for hours it does seem like it's ok to ease off and…

Enough of that sort of thinking, it's a slippery slope. Laura gives me a slice of Soreen from her pack and it's time to distract myself with a longer spell of running, I manage to count to 200 before stopping this time, then 300.

We head across the open expanse of Kings Meadow, and onto a stretch where the railway line swings north-west and squeezes up close to the Thames. The space for the path is now compressed so we're moving along a gloomy corridor hard up against the embankment. There's some to-ing and fro-ing with another runner here. He comes past. I push again and draw level. No-one talks for a while, then Laura tells him well done to break the silence, and his reply sounds weary.

Up the infamously steep steps away from the river just after Tilehurst Station, I try to make it look to Laura as if I can climb them normally, but we have a laugh as I explain stumbling towards the top, that this bravado has come at a cost to my quads.

Although Laura's Strava data showed it had a gradient of about 8 per cent, there's a hill in the housing estate hereabouts that feels to me like the north wall of the Eiger. To add insult to injury someone overtakes us on it. Then we're over the top and jogging back down through Purley-on-Thames to the river at Mapledurham Lock.

We see a lot of Giacomo in his lime green kit again over the next few miles. He's a well-liked, generous competitor who's written a book about his running after recovering from brain surgery (23). I know from our chat at the start that even though he's also going for (and will complete) the

South Downs Way 100 in a few weeks' time, he wanted to be quicker than this. But he still makes time to say something complimentary as we go past.

I'm able to do a couple of running efforts of 6 or 7 minutes through the fields on the way to Whitchurch-on-Thames. We pass the spot Naomi fell in a bog in freezing temperatures and her 2018 race came to an end. I wonder how she's getting on this time and hope she's doing ok.

Then feeling like we've made up some time we're arriving at the narrow single-track bridge at Pangbourne – frequently linked with 'The Wind in the Willows'. Kenneth Grahame lived here for many years and his illustrator based Toad Hall on Mapledurham House – a mile or two back downstream (24).

Up into Whitchurch then, where we meet a woman wearing a fluorescent jacket wrapped up against the now freezing cold; she's the volunteer with the short straw, stood at the end of Manor Road, directing us along the detour to the aid station with a jerky wave of her arm. In the village hall there's a tip off about her, and on the way back, seeing the clock has ticked over into Sunday, me and Laura give her a surprise rendition of happy birthday. She smiles sheepishly.

Then as Laura has got marshalling duties at another race in the morning back in London, it's time to say goodbye, give her a hug and thank her for beyond the call of duty levels of empathy. Then I'm heading off up the hill on my own with my blueberry muesli bar. Time to remember all the work to get this far…

10 A MEAN STREAK

It's a bitter sweet summer.

I'm still struggling to get my head round Dad's death and keep finding myself drawn back to Norfolk – supposedly to do jobs connected with selling Mum and Dad's house – but in reality, because it's a way of being closer to them and I'm not ready to let those feelings go.

At the same time, the powerful 50 mile experience is still in my head. With both parents gone I'm more aware of my own mortality, the discovery there isn't masses of time left. My aspiration to do a 100 mile race hardens, turning into something I've definitely decided to do. My Andy Mouncey book talks about 'performance being emotional' (25) and needing a connection to the ultras you sign up for.

I'm drawn immediately to the Centurion Thames Path 100. It's a point-to-point journey along the river from London to Oxford; the 2019 edition is being held on the same weekend as my 50th birthday; and the race finishes in the place where I was born, less than a mile away from the house in Kennington where our family spent the first four years of my life. It's as if I'm going to be travelling home. I sign up there and then.

June brought a focus on shorter and faster runs and a

new 10k PB on a hilly down-then-back-up course at Heathfield. This impetus carries me through the summer and by September I'm doing 50 miles a week again. Am I peaking too early though? Might it make sense to target a shorter race in the autumn? Stephen Cousins' 'Film My Run' video (26) of the Challenge Running Stort 30 Mile race (27) is appealing and I sign up for it at the end of October.

At the beginning of the month, I spend a week off work on Ithaca in Greece, seeing where Odysseus actually lived. A change is as good as a rest, and it's invigorating to be immersed in the outdoor life, swimming and running up and down hills in the sun every day, looking out over the Ionian Sea.

For the Stort 30 I try to take on board Andy Mouncey's advice around goal setting (28). This isn't just about setting yourself an achievable time goal, it's also deciding how you're going to achieve it. I home in on a target time of 4 hours 40 minutes, realising it by enjoying things, holding my own and racing when possible, and by remembering to have enough to eat and drink.

The race is going well and there's time to reflect on being outside pretty much every day of my 20s, teaching young people how to climb and canoe, then moving in doors to become a professional fundraiser and now spending most days sat at a desk. Running releases me from my responsibilities and takes me back to the great outdoors again.

After nearly two years of week in week out physical effort, it's great to be racing 30 miles in one go, to have nailed the mental preparation necessary for an ultra, to be still moving freely two, three, four hours into a race, with the autumn sun on my face, a feeling of being totally absorbed, exhausted but also exhilarated, forever finding a way to make it to the next bend, to race that canal boat, to smile and still pass a few people as well.

And then picking my way up the hill to the finish, I figure out a faster than expected time of under 4 hours 30 minutes is just about still on, and that it's possible to access the energy and strength to sprint 400 metres round the sports field to the finish. And after, taking it all in, I'm awash with peace and contentment.

A week of recovery follows, then it's time to search for a 100 mile training schedule. Nothing too pushy just a guide to the weekly mileage, how far the back to back weekend long runs need to be. My chosen one is 25 weeks long and peaks at 75 miles a week (29). Ok then, according to my calculations, week one, 40 miles, starts next Monday, 12th November 2018…

Never let it be said that the training is easy, that running after work in November and December isn't hard. The house is warm and comforting especially when it's dark and raining outside. It helps to have a mean streak, a clear objective and a public commitment to it, to kick you into your kit and back out again.

There's a couple of outings in the rain which feel horrible and tedious. Maybe it's because my headtorch is rubbish, time to get a new one – a Petzl Reactiv if you're interested. Suddenly it's like I'm running in the daylight and everything is better for a bit.

Then I get a heavy cold and despite all the advice ever written go out anyway, figuring it's resilience training for when the going gets tough in the 100. Once the cold goes, it starts raining again. One night in the middle of December, it's tipping it down so hard I'm soaked within a few minutes. Later a car drives by just as I'm passing a comically large puddle…

Christmas comes and goes. Then it's time to be puritanical. Up to 58 miles a week for most of January, no alcohol and no meat for a month, and a couple of back to back marathon distance long runs. My commitment to low heart rate workouts slips as I try to do both weekend marathons under 4 hours.

All is going well until the wheels come off in week 13. We're competing for a multi-million contract at work — a one off opportunity to get much needed longer-term funding into about 50 youth clubs. There are about 150 documents to write with very little time. Something's got to give. Trying to do my long run at the weekend, there's nothing in my legs. Zero. Kaput. They're made of concrete. We make the bid deadline though.

A few days later I have to leave a meeting at work as I'm about to start sobbing. Rosemary my boss is there to pick up the pieces and suggests a few days off...

I hole up and hunker down in Mum and Dad's empty holiday bungalow in the Eden Valley along from Penrith. Serendipitously, we haven't managed to sell it yet. After a day or two I feel able to reboot my training and set off for a long run, heading North by West, an old mariner's bearing, underneath the Pennine escarpment. This will be an out and back job. I always carry money on these runs nowadays and spot a little café in Melmerby I can turn into an impromptu aid station on the way back. So I do that and manage marathon distance again.

18 very slow miles the next day and it's 45 miles back to back and 67 for the week. A week or two later I manage my first ever 70+ week and first ever 30 mile long run. There's also a successful and productive recce of the first segment of the race from Richmond to Windsor. Things are back on track....

11 WALKING LIKE FRANKENSTEIN

It's ten past one in the morning and we're over 70 miles into the race. Streatley's wood-panelled village hall is toasty and snug, the mood is soporific, and no-one seems in a hurry to leave. There are some whispered, gallows-humour style exchanges, but mostly intense contemplation, thousand-yard-stare expressions on runners' faces.

Michelle is the volunteer in charge and it's her first time as an aid station 'captain'. It's a way for her to stay involved with the sport while recovering from injury. She and her team are putting in a 12 hour shift through the night to support the entire field of 300 runners. As an experienced ultra runner herself, Michelle can relate to our situation.

She asks if I have everything I need? Her team have topped up my water, helped me get a fresh long-sleeved tee-shirt from my drop bag and made sure I've had enough to eat. Yes, I do actually, thank you. I might as well go back outside and get on with it then. No time like the present.

Back in the dark there is just the one job – carry on moving through the night towards Wallingford, six and a half miles north of here.

My awareness is narrowing still further. Energy is for

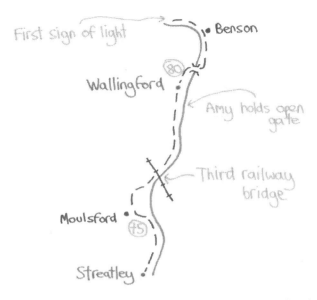

First sign of light   Benson

Wallingford

Amy holds open gate

Third railway bridge

Moulsford

Streatley

essential race-related activity only: keep an eye out for the Centurion marker signs, follow the path ahead as it unfolds in the headtorch beam, walk as fast as you can, run for a count of 100 or 200 when possible, remember slugs of water, take a jelly baby from the shorts pocket when you're getting drowsy.

Occasionally there's the luxury of looking at my Casio watch to try and work out how many hours there are until sunrise – due officially about half five.

It feels surreal being in a race in the middle of the night, and although really sleepy, I'm pleased I got some momentum going on the last leg and seem to be carrying it on now.

I'm following along a vehicle track, then a long open meadow where it's easier to do some running stretches. There's the light of another person a few hundred metres ahead.

Then it's the left hand turn away from the river as we come into Moulsford. Up past some houses then turn right and head along the village for a bit. Trudging uphill I'm hit by a heavy wave of weariness – like suddenly wading through treacle - people are bound to catch me now. No-one does though and there's nothing else to do but plough on.

Back down by the river the route zigzags under another dark and atmospheric railway bridge. I know from my recce, that above me, the mainline west is crossing the Thames for a third and final time, that this is another Brunel job. (A few weeks later I take the train to Bristol to watch the Champions League Final with my brother and crossing this bridge feels almost obscenely fast, the river a sudden flash of silver and light, and then we're accelerating into the straight, off towards Swindon at over hundred miles an hour). Back in the middle of the night, my headtorch picks out the way ahead - across a little boardwalk through on the other side of the bridge.

I'm never completely alone. I've seen quite a lot of a runner called Ben Coleman and his pacer Amy over the last few hours. They're singing and talking to stay awake and although Amy only planned to join him for 20 miles, she'll end up accompanying Ben all the way to Oxford in a bid to keep his sub 24 dream alive. As I jog to the end of a field, Amy has the presence of mind to hold the gate open for me explaining 'you've got a good stride going.' It's a simple act of kindness but at this stage of proceedings resonates for hours. I can only jog on another hundred metres or so more through the wood however and feel guilty slowing to a walk.

It's just after three when I get to the aid station in Wallingford. There are the usual Centurion banners marking the entrance. I stumble down some steps and, with limited motion control, sit down on one of the camping chairs. The last couple of these stops have been in village halls but this one is more like a workshop or garage area. It's been about two hours since Streatley and I am a bit gutted that the air temperature is the same as outside. Someone's scribbled the number 120 on a whiteboard. It must be telling us how many competitors have come through.

In hushed, sympathetic tones a man in his forties – one of the volunteers – asks me if I want a hot drink. Over 17 hours into the race, the fact that this guy is telegraphing empathy when he would normally be asleep means a lot. Time to play my caffeine trump card. I've been avoiding it all day for fear of stomach issues but I'm fighting tiredness, it's been dark for six hours and I need a boost and some warmth. I sip the milky instant coffee for a brief period, struggling to make sense of my surroundings, before reluctantly telling myself sitting down in the cold isn't a great idea. Stand up, make a trip to the loo, then say your thank yous and goodbyes and be off again.

Back out in the street, it's obvious how much my muscles have seized up. I'm walking like Frankenstein, moving very slowly indeed and shivering badly.

I've long since stopped trying to follow my 24 hour schedule but know I've got lots of time before the 28 hour cut off at 1.30pm. Clifton Hampden is eight miles ahead, and in this state, it may well take me three hours, it may be half six by the time I get there.

Allowing room for manoeuvre makes things a bit better. I pour my coffee away and force myself into more of a march. Later I'll realise we just passed a 1,000-year-old castle built by the Normans a stone's throw away (30), but I am more than oblivious to things like that right now. Shortly I'm out of town and back on the path in the darkness, able to contemplate a running effort. By this stage of the night running is a relative term. The only way to do it is to put zero pressure on myself, pick out a flat, compacted section of ground in the headtorch beam, start off with comically slow baby steps and use my arms to develop impetus. Then tell myself I can stop when I've counted to 30. Then find after a few seconds a rhythm does come for a bit. Only for a bit mind.

I'm soon walking again and debating whether to put on my thermal top. It's freezing, but I can't be doing with the faff factor of stopping to get it out of my pack and stripping off. Wracked by indecision and wishing there was someone alongside to help me figure out what to do, this seems like a pivotal moment. Eventually I figure it will probably be even colder to stop and put it on, that the only way to warm up is to speed up. I manage some more running and by Benson Lock I'm moving faster, not shivering any more and through the worst of the rough patch.

A few minutes later I get a reward when looking right there's a faint hint of a lighter tone across the bottom of the eastern horizon. Five minutes later I know I haven't imagined it. It's 3.45 am and starting to get light. To my addled brain this is barely comprehensible. Sunrise isn't until half five. But the earth has made a small but telling tilt towards the sun and the darkness is nearly over....

I'm glad I don't find out until after, that in the hour before dawn the temperature dropped to minus three here on Sunday 5th May, and nearby RAF Benson is a known cold spot in meteorological circles, frequently recording the lowest temperature in England!

12 KINTSUGI

It's the end of March 2019, six weeks before the race. Ilaria and me head over to Florence for her sister's 50th birthday. The training is going well, there are some tell-tale signs of form, and I plan to squeeze in some training around the family get togethers. It's much hillier here than Sussex but that's a minor detail…

One morning, opening the shutters at Ilaria's mum's house, there's birdsong and intense sunlight. It's just before seven in the morning and I feel the urge to run up to the monastery at Monte Senario. We went there in the car a few years ago and I'm drawn by the memory of a spectacular mountain top about five miles away, sweeping panoramic views down to Florence one side and across to the Mugello Valley on the other, which, according to Lorenzo who lives there, forms the backdrop behind the lady in the Mona Lisa.

After training for so long, running sometimes becomes a compulsion, as does the urge to test myself. There are no second thoughts as I set off through the woods with a litre of water and a sketchy idea of where to go and how steep the climb is.

Pick your way across to Olmo and then take the minor road to Bivigliano. Follow the brown 'Santuario' signs and watch for two right turns… After the first, the road rises steadily uphill and I can hear the soft regular thud of my footsteps, my steady breathing in the still mountain air. Sunlight is breaking up the morning mist, giving a translucent quality to the light. I later discover this piece of road is Via Della Casa al Vento, named after the 'house of the wind'.

Another right turn and this time the small single-track road disappears into the distance up a much steeper hill. I begin climbing with an almost literal girding of the loins, instructing myself not to stop even if the road is like this for the remaining two miles or so up to the monastery. The route unfolds upwards through a soft pastoral landscape. It's almost as if I am ascending into heaven. Despite the effort there's that invigorating feeling you often get when you're running in a new place – discovery, freedom and endorphins coming together to create a potent mix.

The road veers round a hairpin to the right, entering the cooler pine forest that covers the top of the peak. I need to be back by half eight and only have 10 minutes or so before it's time to turn around. Yet still the road climbs steeply uphill. I'm fighting for breath and sweat is streaming into my eyes as I push to try and reach the top before the cut off. Eventually with only a few seconds to spare I make a final right turn and can see 400 metres or so of very steeply ramped road up to the monastery.

Relieved, I chug up to the top and have a breather before setting off home. Encouraged by the thrill of the climb, I let my speed increase on the way down and begin to move faster and faster. On the steepest part of the descent there's that uncontrolled rush you get when you're at maximum velocity. And then inevitably, almost imperceptibly at first, I feel something shift inside my right knee, and there's a sense of déjà vu…

Dr Tim Noakes describes the first phase of injury as denial (31). Limping on for a couple more runs, I'm a textbook example of this phase, before realising the very sharp pain in the top of my knee is telling me to stop.

On the first day back in England I'm knocking down the door of my osteopath – Nick Tuckley has worked miracles in the past and now I need one again. The session goes well, and there's the sense of things moving back into place - although it's uncomfortable the knee does feel better.

That weekend after four days without running, I try a mile round the block. There's a twinge but no pain. Then against Ilaria's advice, against Nick's advice, against the yoga teacher's advice I go for a longer run. Even the cat raises an eyebrow. I don't want to lose my form, I don't want to fall any further behind the training plan, I won't be told. After five miles it's ok, six the same. I pass a woman and a girl with a horse who say I look like I could run forever. Ego, damn ego. I push on for another loop and then the sharp pain comes back and it's a struggle to hobble home.

Over the next few days icing the knee and struggling to walk, it's as if I've dropped a very expensive vase, smashing it into thousands of tiny little pieces. All that work, all that training, all that effort and now it looks as though the race isn't going to happen. I'm beating myself up a fair bit that week.

They say it's the hope that kills you. The only way to cope is to tell myself I won't be doing the 100 mile race, to concentrate on getting over the injury. 11 days go by without a run. I go back to see Nick, rest and ice the knee.

Despite my best efforts, a chink of hope does creep back in. By Saturday 13th April, three weeks before the day of the race the knee is less uncomfortable. I figure it might be possible to kill two birds with one stone. Try an exploratory long run ready to stop at the first sign of trouble, and recce some of the night section of the course at the same time. Just in case you get to do the race. Park up at Reading Station and very slowly and very gingerly start jogging west.

One mile without pain becomes two, then five, then hallelujah, ten. I make it through to Streatley, get lost in

Moulsford, push ever so gently on past Agatha Christie's old house (32) to Wallingford. I ring Ilaria and tell her all is ok, that I might go further. I stop for some water and food then carry on up the Thames Path past Benson and Shillingford and onto a remote stretch along by Little Wittenham Nature Reserve where I hear my first cuckoo, where it's just me and the sheep and the early evening light, where with only the river for company, I feel like the last man in England. After 30 miles and 5 hours I eventually stop at Culham. The knee is ok. It seems like the most important run I've ever done.

The week after it's Easter and a long weekend, but no time with Dad any more. Using the surprisingly extensive train network criss-crossing the Thames, which he would have briefed me on at length, I manage to recce the three remaining bits of the race - Windsor to Marlow, Marlow to Reading, and with 11 days to go, the last leg from Culham to Oxford.

I get accustomed to some typical Thames tableaux: the desirable riverside residences, clearly architect designed; the queues of cruisers either side of the pound locks decked out with chattering Chablis drinkers; and on the fringes of the bigger towns, the water meadows peopled with families and couples taking a leisurely passeggiata in the sun.

And the recces have undoubtedly been helpful in terms of mental preparation. I can now visualise the whole course and am very unlikely to get lost. But there has been an unintended consequence. I've seen first-hand just how far one hundred miles is on foot. Each of the five runs has been a tough day out in its own right. Now it's time to put them all together.

Having got over the knee injury, in the last week before the race I start tying myself in knots with anxiety. I have created this seemingly impossible challenge for myself, everyone knows all about it and there is no way to back down, nowhere to hide. There's a stress-like sensation building in the bottom of my stomach.

It doesn't feel right to relax, it doesn't feel right to sleep - we won't be able to do that in the race. I am worried about the hours of darkness, having not gone a whole night without sleep for about 30 years. I make a list of all the things that can go wrong, stopping at 24 thinking I've made things worse.

Around me people are saying reassuring things, but I can't connect with their words or gain any comfort from them. I am in a separate place - like an isolation ward or about to face a rites of passage experience or something. A storm is coming and all I can do is wait for it to hit.

I know how much I'll beat myself up if I fail. I've spent years not giving myself any credit for the first marathon because I failed to achieve my sub 3.30 goal. And the weekend before the race following the Andy Mouncey advice, I'd pushed myself to create a sub 24 hour timing schedule. For each of the 14 legs I have a target pace, and for each aid station a maximum number of minutes I can stop. This schedule is creating more worry. How will I react if I fall behind? Am I being too ambitious? Is it right to target sub 24? Am I setting myself up to fail? I know I can let the negative voice have the upper hand if I've fall behind in a race.

And when I dream about running, it frequently tends to be an anxiety dream. I'm sprinting along in a race, excitingly ahead of schedule, when something goes wrong. Maybe the route mysteriously veers into a house, along a corridor and into what becomes an increasing dead end, locked doors and no way out, no way to figure out where to go next as the minutes tick away. Or I'm up near the front and gradually my thigh muscles turn to lead, and I can't propel myself forward with any speed. There have been times in races like Milton Keynes when it felt like I ran like the wind or in the 50 miler when I could run forever. Why can't I dream about that!

In those final few days before the race, the negative voice

in my head held me in its power and I couldn't break back into positive thinking.

I'd spent time in therapy, attempting to understand more about this voice. And why – amongst other things - it would always be pushing me coldly to do more. Why was I always striving so hard?

Why had I come up with the idea of the 35 mile walk, why had I felt the need to go to K2 - to such a faraway inhospitable place when I wasn't ready for it, why had I driven myself so hard in marathon training in 2006. Come to think of it, why wasn't 100 miles enough, why did I have to try and do it within 24 hours first time around? Why was it never enough?

One session I finally figured out where this impulse to repeatedly push myself came from. I wanted to make my Dad proud. Whatever I did, whatever I managed to achieve I was always trying to get recognition from him. And this recognition always felt tantalisingly out of reach. So I'd push myself harder.

I remember telling the therapist - 'and it's never enough, it's never enough.' I started to cry and then to sob. The tears came in a flood, from a place so deep inside me, I never knew it existed before, as if from the bottom of a well.

It didn't give me a cure from this compulsion but at least I had some understanding of it…

Maybe it takes some of us a lifetime to figure out and own up to our broken bits.

In the Happiness Dictionary, Dr Tim Lomas talks about 'a process of ceramic repair known as 'kintsugi' – literally 'golden joinery.' Rather than throwing out their broken pots and bowls, practitioners of this art apply seams of gold lacquer to the pieces and reassemble them with love and care' (33). The cracks are deliberately highlighted rather than hidden away. This approach is sometimes used by psychologists and psychotherapists to help people overcome trauma and adversity.

Even though he was no longer here, this desire to try

and make my Dad proud, to always be pushing myself harder in the process, had undoubtedly encouraged me to try and run 100 miles. Although this drive had an unhelpful, compulsive side to it, if the kintsugi principle worked, maybe something good could come from it. After all running away from rejection had led to Milton Keynes; and a journey that began with trying to escape my grief, had ended up on the coast path near Minehead…

There's one day to go before the Thames Path race, Ilaria encourages me to go to a yoga class up the road in Uckfield.

Lying on the floor on my mat, I immediately feel earthed, the sensation of being physically grounded. Grace is the teacher. I like Grace. She doesn't take herself too seriously, her humour is never very far below the surface, but she does takes yoga seriously, as well as the wisdom underneath it. It's not just what she says, it's how she says it.

She tells us the session is about self-awareness — being aware of your thoughts but not beholden to them. When we are mindful, we have the opportunity to connect to the divine, and everyone has the divine in them…

These insights come at just the right time. It's as if the advice is directed at me and I make a pact with myself to be self-aware during the race. I come out of the session calmer and ready to pack my kit for the morning

13 PERFORMANCE IS EMOTIONAL

Back on the trail between Wallingford and Clifton Hampden we're experiencing a rather special dawn.

It's as if the sky is like a giant kaleidoscope. Every time I look up, the earth has turned a tiny bit more, the colours have been shaken up again and all the roses and violets and blues rearranged. It's a natural light show that's there every morning, but something about journeying for so long on foot, being out in nature all this time, moving continuously through the long, cold night, gives this daybreak a new intensity, a power and serenity beyond anything I've experienced before.

Crossing the footbridge at Day's Lock, I can see all the crews again, lined up along the path on the far bank. Then when I get over there they've mysteriously disappeared. So I'm hallucinating, and your point is? The rules are being rewritten moment by moment right now!

During the night the river was dark and foreboding, an abyss on our left, then right hand side. Now just before sunrise it's in a more tranquil mood - the freezing mist rising from it is like dry ice and indigo in colour, and the Thames itself is milky in tone and going about its business

completely oblivious to our efforts.

Speaking of which as well as I'm doing, Clifton Hampden isn't in sight yet. It may be serendipitous that my headtorch ran out of batteries just at the point it became light enough to properly see, but in other news, this left hand bend in the river has been going on forever. Where's the bridge across to the aid station? Why do we need so many gates suddenly? Why is the trail so uneven along here? Those houses must be the beginning of Clifton Hampden. No, they're not, they're a completely unconnected village called Burcot. As you were. Why do all the ligaments at the back of my knees seem like they've been replaced with steel cables? Why have my feet expanded and been squeezed into running shoes a few sizes too small? Why is even walking hard right now?

What seems like an age later the bridge we need to cross finally comes into view. I'm afraid I couldn't care less about its six beautiful Tudor arches (34). There's now a tedious five minute detour, a compulsory walk away from the path to check in at the aid station in Clifton Hampden village hall. Right then, grab some handfuls of the usual savoury and sweet suspects and stuff them in. Things have clearly gone a bit better than the half past six worst case scenario I worried about back in Wallingford; but let's not take stock until I'm through the village and re-established at the river. On the way back there's a glimpse of Helen and Spencer, still together, still focused and pushing hard.

Back by the Thames my trusty Casio reads 5.28am. Culham is three miles further on. I set myself a goal of getting there by 06.15. I'm concentrating on the trail ahead, all rutted and narrow now, as it follows along the edges of fields of crops. I repeatedly instruct myself to avoid tripping over, to not twist an ankle, to shut out all the complaining from those badly deteriorated, increasingly angry muscle groups.

Ok think. I need to do each mile in a quarter of an hour. My legs won't let me walk faster than 20 minutes per mile. And 10 minutes per mile is the speediest I can possibly run. Even my tired brain can handle these maths. I need to be running at least fifty per cent of the time.

Running is easier said than done. It requires increasingly vigorous use of my arms to force a kind of spluttered jogging action - like pulling out the choke on our tangerine-coloured 70s Ford Escort as it neared the end of its life. My swinging, funky-chicken limbs eventually come together in remembered energy, coalesce into more than the sum of their parts, and my body starts to run of its own accord.

I've got this far by not putting pressure on myself but I'm finding it increasingly hard to ignore my fall back plan for finishing the race inside one day – the final push home from Culham.

I get there two minutes early and it's time to stop kidding myself. I'm definitely going for it. I remember a quote from my Andy Mouncey book 'the ones that remain? They are the ones who want it!' (35) I want it alright, I've come 88 miles, got through Dad's death, run week after week for two years, recovered from injury, had sleepless nights for a week. And I know from the brief check of my phone at Henley that there's a few people rooting for dot number 58 on the tracker. Performance is emotional. Time to stand up and be counted, lay everything on the line.

Around me everything is waking up. After the cold of the night, the rising sun is starting to bring a hint of warmth to the day; along with the chatter of birdsong, my sense of smell is triggered for the first time in ages by the heady scent of spring on the breeze.

And here twenty-one hours into the race, I've reached the moment of maximum effort. I might have started all this running to get away from feelings of inadequacy and loneliness, to get away from grief, forever trying to prove a point to the tiresome nagging voice in my head telling me I need to be giving it everything. But that's no longer the case. Not any more. I'm somewhere new now, out the other side into completely different territory, and dare I say it, as close to fulfilment as it's possible to be. A small part of me is able to savour how amazing this is. And that I don't want this journey to end…

Just before quarter to seven I'm approaching Abingdon. There's a small woman forever a hundred metres or so ahead of me who's got a decent tempo going. I've been working hard for ages to try and catch her but to no avail. At least she seems to be pulling me along.

I'm worried there'll be another detour to the aid station but luckily, it's just by the path. Lou is volunteering here and she's an experienced ultra runner herself, she knows competitors coming through at this point have got a one day belt buckle in their sights. 'Passing through?' she shouts. 'Number 58' I shout back. 'We've got your number!' comes her reply.

Over the walkway at Abingdon Lock. Speed march through the woods. Then back along by the river and run for a count of 100 when you can. Repeat, then repeat again. And again. I spy with my little eye, a railway bridge, a country house on the right, the Lower Radley boathouses.

And as per the last 95 miles, the Centurion marker tape and signs are forever in place seamlessly showing us the way. I'm taking them for granted right now but find out afterwards a guy called Ivor Hewitt put them in place along here. Ivor was half-way through running all four 100 mile races in 2018 when he was almost killed in a cycling accident in the City of London. He's nearly recovered now, using marking duties as a stepping stone and will be back running ultras in 2020.

My watch says quarter to eight. The 24 hour cut off is at half nine so there's an hour and three-quarters to do four and a half miles or so. I can't do those maths. Or can I. It must be over 20 minutes per mile. I finally admit to myself that there's time in the bank, that the 24 hour belt buckle is in reach. But everything is close to breaking point, I might get cramp, an Achilles or knee might stop working completely, I must push on.

Another runner passes with a bit of a see-you-later attitude, a bit of an edge. I speed up and pass him back. He grins as he returns the favour a minute or two later. Damn!

My running efforts are getting rarer. The landmarks start to feel like they might be triggering old childhood memories, but they're buried just too deep. Here's a familiar looking set of pylons, Sandford Lock where I'm told we used to come and play, another railway bridge, then Iffley Lock. Not far from here Sir Roger Bannister's effort only lasted a smidge under four minutes – lightweight! (36)

I'm definitely on the outskirts of Oxford now. Locals are out for their Sunday run, way faster than me. There's an eight on the river, their coach accelerating past me on his bike shouting about the finish. Speaking of which, surely that's the corner before Hinksey stream where I'll be able to see the boathouses? Isn't that Ila filming me with her iPad? Here's the turn into Queens College Sports Ground and the blue inflatable arch marking the finish line. The grass is soft and flat and cool. I find I can pick my knees up and still run.

There's so much packed into these last few seconds it's

almost impossible to experience them all at once.

It may have been me that's gone the distance, but there are so many others who've been part of this, who've made it a collective effort. Pete pulled together all the maps for the 50 mile race. Ilaria had hot food ready for me when I got back from training runs. Rosemary's three-year-old daughter Erin waited patiently to wave to me at Teddington. There was the ham sandwich maker at Wraysbury, the lady with the pasta at Henley, the guy who made me a coffee at Wallingford. Fi and Tony and Rachel and many others have had my back when I'm running. All those dot watchers have been hitting refresh and willing it to get a wiggle on. That's just the tip of the iceberg. And Mum and Dad of course. Not around anymore to be part of this. But deeply connected with this place and with me and my struggle. And somewhere close by.

Just the last few strides... And then I get to finally cross the line and stop the clock on 23 hours, 25 minutes and 42 seconds. James Elson shakes my hand and gives me a one day belt buckle. Ila gives me a hug. I can stop now.

Incidentally, every year crowds of nearly a million turn up on the streets of London to watch the marathon. In contrast here in Oxford there are eight or nine people giving me polite applause at the finish. I like that about ultras. It's humbling, keeps us honest. And stops us getting big headed!

14 AFTERMATH

And after?

I hadn't really thought about after…

Alex was there at the finish. He'd got his one day buckle too and we had a celebratory bacon butty together.

Ilaria helped me back to the car and was on hand to beep our horn with exuberant excitement as, running on fumes, Ben Coleman dug deep to come sprinting across the line a few seconds before the clock ticked over onto 24 hours. His pacer Amy was still by his side. In a typical example of attention to detail, one of the Centurion team had gone down the towpath to find Ben and tell him 'you've got half a mile to go and six minutes to do it. Get moving!'

Spencer and Helen made it in together under 24 hours, both for the first time. Giacomo got a one day buckle too. There was a typically gutsy performance from Naomi who finally completed her first 100 mile race. As did Brian, whose children were there to complete the last few metres with him.

They're all still running – Giacomo was out the day after, maintaining his run streak. Incredibly, in August, he still had the stamina to win the Hell on the Humber 36 hour race.

The debate about whether it was 102 or 103 miles was

never settled. There were 224 finishers in all.

My phone was filled with notifications – encouraging videos from Hindleap instructors, tweets and texts from friends and colleagues, Facebook posts, my siblings keeping up with things on the WhatsApp group.

Laura had made a massive difference during the first part of the night and I texted her to tell her I'd made it and to say thank you. And Clare too – who'd had to take her fruitcake home.

I'd been so wrapped up in the race itself I genuinely hadn't thought about how I would feel afterwards. For 36 hours the pain in my legs was too great to sleep and once that subsided both knees were very sore. Ilaria picked up the pieces and found me some medicinal cannabis oil and compression socks that took the edge off things, but it was four weeks before I felt ready to run again. Alex had a similar experience and said it took him about six weeks. While I've been intentionally evangelical about the benefits of a 100 mile race, I would recommend other first timers learn from my mistake and read up more in advance about how to manage the recovery phase (37). Centurion send all runners detailed notes about this.

Psychologically though, I felt like I had made a once in a lifetime effort, like I'd seen the far side of the moon, discovered this deep reservoir of positive emotion that wouldn't ever go away. I was struggling to find the right way to describe how it felt. In the Happiness Dictionary Dr Tim Lomas offers a first-rate expression from Mandarin - the expression 'xìng fú'. Contentment that feels hard won, happiness experienced after battling through adversity (38). As someone who'd had the protestant work ethic drilled into me through my childhood, this appealed to my puritanical side.

I still wanted to know more though, to understand why the race had gone better than expected, why it had been such a compelling experience.

Over 10 intense days in Greece - writing down the story and thinking through the experience – I began to piece things together.

There's one image I can't get out of my head. Maybe all that anxiety the week before the race was like shaking up a fizzy bottle, and during the event itself the top was well and truly off, and all my restless energy could finally be channelled somewhere. Maybe what I was calling anxiety was actually my mind doing the heavy lifting in advance, gearing itself up for the challenge ahead.

There was the crucial and timely advice from yoga teacher Grace, flagging the benefits of being self-aware, helping calm my state of mind for the race. As a result, I was ready to spot the dehydration before Wraysbury, see the advantages of slowing down and walking out of aid stations to digest food, and figure ditching the GPS watch might be a good thing.

Looking back at my list of the 24 things that could go wrong, it read more positively after the race as an action plan for unexpected scenarios. For example, as well as hunger knock and getting lost, I had written 'things going better than expected,' and alongside in the how to respond column, suggested 'be aware of my competitive spirit and use it.' And I had remembered to do this, especially during the rain showers; on the section between Whitchurch and Streatley which built momentum for the rest of the night; and on the push to the finish. The mental preparation that went into putting that list together was worth it.

And in the longer stretches between aid stations when it was a case of just having to endure, one part of my preparation had made a difference – a tendency to seek out extra challenges above and beyond the training schedule. Running up Snowdon; discovering an extra hillier loop to add to the run to work; doing a circuit of Ithaca on my first day on the island; carrying on with a 28 mile long run through the middle of Storm Freya. I don't give these examples for reasons of machismo but because I think seeking out adversity helps to condition the 'Central Governor' (39), the voice in your head that cautions restraint, that you can cope with the unexpected, you are going to carry on whether they like it or not.

The race also taught me I spend so much time thinking about the things that can go wrong there's a risk I forget to plan properly for, and enjoy, things going right. In the middle of a low point in my early 30s, my brother-in-law Andrew had talked to me about finding my potency. This advice had stayed with me and over the 100 miles I believe I found it.

I was drawn back to Mihaly Csikszentmihalyi's book 'Flow: The Psychology of Happiness' (40). He researched the positive benefits of being totally focused and immersed in an activity. When I did the Master's degree in Edinburgh and looked into the spiritual side of outdoor education, I'd discovered his work and found it illuminating. I'd seen through climbing and canoeing how you could become totally absorbed in a task, how this turns off the tyrannical chatter of your inner voice and helps create powerful experiences.

You might become intensely focused on your next handhole, a rugosity of rock the size of a thumbnail, if pulling on it from the right direction helps you make your next move hundreds of feet up a climb. Or kayaking through a challenging rapid in the heart of a Scottish wild wood, amidst the unpredictable buffeting of the icy, peat-coloured water, the paddle becomes an extension of your limbs and you escape a near certain capsize with a support stroke that happens without thinking.

Similarly, I had spent much of the 100 miles completely wrapped up in what I was doing: following the undulations and feel of the trail; preferring to be in my world rather than that of the pub dwellers at Henley; increasingly absorbed in the race, not wanting it to end. Csikszentmihalyi's description of how flow comes about, all correspond with the ultra running experience – 'the challenging activity; the merging of action and awareness; clear goals and feedback; concentration; the possibility of control; the loss of self-consciousness; and the transformation of time' (41).

I think checking out the course in advance contributed to this. I had it all buried in my brain and there were long periods when the next bend in the path, the next meadow or scene change unspooled seamlessly like it was meant to be. And in the second half of the race after ditching the GPS watch I was even more absorbed, after hundreds of hours of running I could judge my speed better than I gave myself credit for, but it meant I had to concentrate more.

Csikszentmihalyi does offer a note of caution that this type of experience 'can become addictive' (42) – a reflection 22 hour Richard, who's describes himself as now 'hooked on running' (see below), might agree with; other ultra runners have soulfully picked up on this too (43). Is now the time for me to own up to some ambiguity around reaching the finish line? Stepping back out of the race bubble wasn't easy because the experience had been so intense, and normal life was bound to be less straightforward.

As well as the Flow experience, there was also the moment towards the end, just after the sun rose, when I was going as hard as I could, and felt 'as close to fulfilment as it's possible to be'. I was still me, with all my flaws and insecurities, but it felt like a more complete me than normal, someone close to my best possible self. I had found peace and was finally living without fear. There was a coherence to my efforts and place in the world, a rightness and unity in that moment that would always stay with me. It was a natural culmination of what had gone before and a source of hope for the future.

I am convinced much of what I felt overlaps with what

Abraham Maslow calls a peak experience – a unifying, defining moment above and beyond every day events. In 'Religions, Values and Peak Experiences' he argues these transcendental experiences have traditionally been the preserve of the major religions, which has done the rest of us a disservice – this sort of self-actualising experience should be open to everyone (44).

Longer ultras offer a lengthy period of being in tune with one's body, an immersion in the natural environment; they come at the end of a period of intense preparation, and they push participants to find a way to reach deeply into their physical and psychological reserves. I believe they offer a fertile hunting ground for those in search of their own peak experience.

They are also richly communal, shared experiences. Ben Coleman subsequently told me he was a different person after the race, that he genuinely believed it changed people's lives. As other runners movingly shared their accounts through the summer, the power of our collective experience was amplified still further. I've included these accounts below.

And finally, through the conversations and messages afterwards, it became apparent that my brother Ian, who was with me on our unofficial ultra across the Lakes, who has overcome a lot of adversity in his life, who has started running too in the last few months training for his first park run, had been watching my dot for most of the 24 hours. He even spotted that I made up a few places during the night. It was in the end, too late for Dad, but I was choked to realise Ian might actually be proud of me.

STORIES FROM OTHER RUNNERS AND VOLUNTEERS

I think my Ultra journey was always going to end with a 100 miler somewhere because I like even numbers. It just makes sense doesn't it? 26.2 is a completely arbitrary figure. 50 is good but 100. It just looks good doesn't it? And to do 100 miles in 24 hours would be special...

I had done quite a few marathons and shorter ultras before TP100 mainly in an attempt to alleviate my mid-life crisis but then started reading about heroic 100 milers like Scott Jurek, Ann Trason, Jim Walmsley and Kilian Jornet. (I'd actually like to imagine myself as a fatter, older version of Zach Miller - go out too fast, tire then end each race dramatically). I just had to have a go. I had no real idea of my limits before TP100 but loved the idea of trying to find where they were.

I felt fit, ready and reasonably confident at the start but, my god, it was a hard 24 hours. I kept a decent pace for the first half and reached Henley in a good time and felt in ok shape. I met some lovely people along the way, and we shared stories of our lives, experiences and races. The miles slowly ticked away.

At Reading, I met my wife, Abbie, and my pacer, Amy. Amy was only going to join me for 20 miles, but we soon fell into a rhythm and we just kept plodding along together until the end. I genuinely couldn't have done it without her and along with the standard medal and a t-shirt I gained something better - a good friend. We ran, we walked, we got lost, we talked, we sang, we froze in the night, I cried into my salted caramel Gu gels until I could barely move a muscle.

Daylight arrived and Oxford came closer when a friendly Centurion marshall called out to me "You've got half a mile to go and 6 minutes to do it. Get moving!" We realised that a 24 hour finish was a possibility, so my legs went into a kind of automatic wobbly sprint mode. I made it. 23 hours 59 minutes and 35 seconds.

Looking back, I realise how much I loved every single minute of the training, the prep and the running. James Elson and the whole Centurion team put on an extraordinary race that genuinely changes lives. I am undoubtedly a different person since I took up the 100 mile challenge. In fact, I'm doing it again next year!

Ben Coleman

There was a sense of inevitability that I would run 100 miles at some stage. I quit drink and drugs in 2008 and from the moment I first put on a pair of running shoes in 2012 I was hooked. It enabled me to fill the huge amount of time I found I had but was also a way to get a far safer rush of endorphins. After all I am and will always be an addict. My road to 100 miles has been a progressive one as I graduated from marathons and worked through the various ultra distances, always with a cry of 'never again'. The Thames Path was really the culmination of two years of running. Without doubt the toughest challenge I've taken on but also the day I learnt I can endure and succeed in ways I never thought possible, lessons that I know will stand me in good stay not just for my future adventures but also in life itself. If you can get through 100 miles you can pretty much suffer through anything.

Richard Bridgewater

My first attempt at a 100 miler was the 2018 Thames Path 100. A stress fracture had seen me out of action for the summer of 2017 and I wanted a big target to focus on for my return to running. Sadly *my attempt ended around mile 65 when I fell into a bog and had to be rescued by two lovely ladies who walked me to the aid station at Whitchurch.*

But the 100 mile bug was still there and 12 months later I was back on the start line at Richmond, much better prepared for what was to come. At the finish, after running 26:06:06, I swore never again. But that resolve hasn't lasted and I'm already targeting another Centurion event in 2020 – the Autumn 100 which combines the Thames Path with The Ridgeway. Centurion really do put on the best events – the best organisation, the best volunteers and such a wonderful spirit among the runners. I fear I am addicted – but what a great group of people to share my addiction with.

Naomi Amor

This race was my first 100 miler after managing, somehow, to complete the Centurion 50 Slam the year before. I didn't even want to do a 100 because it's a ridiculous distance, the finish rates are low even amongst seasoned pros and it absolutely batters your body. However, the siren song of "100 miles" seems to call for most ultra runners at some point. It wasn't a perfect race, it was simultaneously harder and easier than I was expecting, but expectations when you're stepping from 50 to 100 miles are pointless. A finish is a finish regardless of time (26:49) and the memories last a lifetime.

Brian Drought

Thames Path was my second 100 mile event, after a tough Autumn 100 in 2017 and just about making the cut off with 20 minutes to spare I felt I was ready to learn from the experience and go again, this time with a goal of finishing within 24 hours.

The morning went off easily, I felt very relaxed and grateful to see some friendly faces on the start line. One thing I had learnt from the first time was to never think of the overall distance, for me that's just too overwhelming - but to stay in that exact moment; plod, plod, plod, one foot in front of the other.

That said, I did take a tumble in the first 30 miles from not watching my feet and daydreaming – and judging from the concerned faces at the checkpoints to follow I think this looked worse than it felt.

Just before the halfway point in Henley, Spencer caught up with me and knowing we both had the same time goal we then stuck together for the rest of the race. Not only did this come at just the right time for me (I was starting to think running on your own could be very lonely for 24 hours), Spencer had a run/walk pace set on his watch, so we soon got into a good rhythm from here until the finish - although there were times when I protested the running had come around way too quickly!

There's so much about running a long distance that is hard, and so much that starts to hurt. But I truly believe, that along with eating and drinking enough, once you have accepted the pain you can keep going and going and going.

Because once it's done and the battle is won all I ever remember is the special, peaceful darkness, the revitalising sunrise, the beauty of the route and the camaraderie between the runners and the volunteers. Friendships are forged through running, but nothing like the bond made between runners on those dark trails through the night, over the party buffet in the checkpoints – even seeing a light from a headtorch bobbing behind you makes you feel like you are in good company.

This isn't supposed to be a club but once you know you know. The sense of achievement is immense, just for 24 hours all you need in life is packed in that little bag on your back.

Helen Wyatt

This was my fifth attempt at a 100 and I was currently two won two lost. I had done TP100 in 2017 in 26hrs 37mins and this was my first 100. 2019 was my first sub 24 in 23hrs 40mins.

Spencer Millberry

I first found out about the Thames Path 100 in 2017 when I volunteered to find out more about ultras and got hooked. Up to that point I had only run one marathon but knew this was a path I wanted to take. In 2018 I ran it and desperately wanted sub 24hrs but ended up wasting a lot of time in aid stations. 2019 meant getting THAT buckle and I knew that if I was effective through aid stations I would get it. I put everything in to training to achieve my goal and was so relieved to finish with a little time to spare. The race took everything out of me and I wasn't running properly until around 6 weeks afterwards but it was so worth it!

Alex Lee

The whole team were there at Streatley from about 6pm on the Saturday through until about 6.30pm Sunday morning - a 12 hour shift overall.

I personally volunteered for a couple of reasons. I moved into ultras very quickly (first 100k after five months of running) and my first 100 along the North Downs Way in 2015 was a real eye opener – after two and a half years running. That was a total pain fest and the Centurion volunteers on that event were amazing, so I wanted to do some volunteering to give back after that. Then I ran the Autumn 100 in 2018 with some injuries so I had to take time off to recover – a year off races - so it was also a way of still being involved, and with a company that has a very well-deserved positive reputation.

I had volunteered at the South Downs Way 50 mile race in 2018 and 2019 and it surprised me how much I enjoyed helping others, as I'd always assumed, I would be annoyed and frustrated at not being able to run the race instead. And of course friends I've made through running and Centurion races and the Facebook group, were participating so I wanted to be there to encourage them too.

I've been very lucky to run in some great races, in some amazing places in this world, and a huge part of those experiences (including the dark places which we always hit in the long dark miles) are very much highlighted by the people who are around us, for me at least. To be able to help others, to be empathetic, motivating, and also tough enough to push someone who isn't in a great place… and then when you find out they hit their goal, it's an amazing feeling and a privilege to be a small part of it

Michelle Payne

I love Centurion events, James and the team, so after racing at some, I volunteered a few times and helped out at aid stations, but I really preferred being outside and moving, which is why I got into marking....

2018 was my going to be my grand slam year [doing all four Centurion 100 mile races]. Things were going smoothly but then after doing the first two, at the end of July I nearly died in a cycling accident on the commute home from work....

I had to regroup and re-evaluate. I tried to get racing again, but it just wasn't happening. I missed the atmosphere, the events, the locations, the people. I dropped a line to James and knowing that I know all the courses and had proved my ability marking – he lined me up for marking duties at all of the 100's this year.

The Thames Path marking was rather eventful. When you're marking you move at about three miles per hour. I had a system with a big rucksack with arrows in one section, zip ties in another pocket, tape in another, all good. So I'm trotting along perfectly on pace, spotting signs to mark-up and places to tape. Then just before Radley, I reach into my bag and find all the cable ties have bounced out. I haven't got enough left to finish. I hunt around, send a quick message to Centurion to let them know, then double back and search for a few miles. But the cable ties could have bounced out anywhere and there's no sign. After some Googling I figure out where there's an industrial park and head towards it, hunting around I locate a Halfords, buy a massive box of ties, and head back to where I left the course. sorted.

Ivor Hewitt

THANK YOU

Like many other people, when I first heard the audio of pilot Chesley Sullenberger's matter of fact response to air traffic control - 'we're going to be in the Hudson' — it triggered some primeval part of my brain, made the hairs on the back of my neck stood up....

'Sully' has quite rightly been lauded as a hero, a case study of resilience and calm under pressure ever since. But he's always been quite modest and self-effacing about that day, emphasizing that the overall disaster response was dependent on a huge number of people. The cabin crew helped stay calm and professional and reassured the passengers - hearing this comforted and steadied him; the emergency services had the presence of mind to mobilise on the side of the river closest to the hospital facilities; the air traffic controllers were instantaneously on the case on his behalf (45).

I wouldn't for a second want to compare running an ultra to saving the lives of 155 people, but Sully's view on what actually happened to US Airways Flight 1549 matters because it shows when we reduce human endeavour down to just one person, we forget about an essential part of our condition — our absolute dependence on one another. Running an ultra may seem individualistic but it so isn't. I couldn't have begun to do it on my own.

So a sincere thank you to...

...Ilaria who always gave me her love and support and patience.

…*James Elson and the Centurion team who absolutely understand what it's like to run an ultra and bend over backwards to create a spot on race experience.*

…*Every single Centurion volunteer including Michelle, Lou, and Ivor. Many were ultra runners themselves; all showed levels of empathy which amplify one's faith in human nature, offer hope that we will all end up ok.*

…*The other #TP100 runners including Giacomo Squintani, Richard Bridgewater, Spencer Millberry, Helen Wyatt, Alex Lee, Naomi Amor and Brian Drought who fed back on the book, and generously let me share their stories; Nick who shared his running and walking strategy, and Stephen Cousins who provided competitive stimulus between Whitchurch and Streatley and inspired me through his films.*

…*My brother Ian, and sisters Heather and Louise who pulled together after Dad died, who were always supportive, and gave helpful feedback on the book.*

…*Everyone who came along to support during the race – including Ilaria; Laura; Rosemary and Erin; Scott Holland; and Clare.*

…*Nic and Rach who came to support me during the 50 mile race, turning up at the most perfect moment. And Jon Penrice too for his companionship through Bridgewater.*

…*Nick Tuckley the osteopath and Grace the yoga teacher who gave invaluable practical help.*

…*Running buddies including: PK who famously beat me onto the Golden Gate bridge in San Francisco; my pal Dr Paolo Molino with whom I shared some memorable runs in Greece and Italy; Michael Beckmann who just nailed his first half marathon; Alan Routledge the heart rate guru who was there at the Stort 30; Liz who I haven't run with yet but who lets me talk about running incessantly; Lee who I'm certain is going to do a 100 mile race one day soon.*

…*All my supportive colleagues at London Youth including Tony Smith who I am proud to count as a friend; Fi and Pete who think I'm mad but who always listened to my running stories and had my back; Laura and Toby and the two Toms and everyone else at Hindleap who got into the dot watching and sent messages of support; Kawika with his Henry V quote*

...Professor Andrew Cooper, Laura Blazey (again), Christine Bass, Amy Galvin-Elliott (again), Sally Marsh, Ivor Hewitt and Phillip Kerry who all gave very helpful feedback on the book. Andrew suggested the Sully analogy.

...Ursula at Sonnenseite, and Laura and Barbara from Turin who supported the book writing efforts in Greece.

...And definitely finally for good this time, when I wasn't writing in Greece, and it was cool enough, I'd go out for a run. I was often joined by a dog we christened Spotty, a local stray. Spotty couldn't believe his luck when he discovered someone else in his town liked running too. Trotting through air thick with the scent of wild thyme, he'd stay ahead of me, checking back from time to time to make sure we were both headed in the same direction, his tail rotating in a wide, carefree circle, with what looked like a massive grin on his face - as though he was having the time of his life, as though he could go forever. Spotty loved running and I tried to capture a little of his spirit when writing. I'm very grateful to him too.

REFERENCES

1.   For example, Andy Mouncey, 'So you want to run an ultra' (Marlborough: Crowood Press, 2014)

2.   I'm thinking in particular of Scott Jurek's 'Eat & Run' (London: Bloomsbury, 2012) and Dean Karnazes 'Ultra Marathon Man: Confessions of an All-Night Runner' (London: Allen & Unwin, 2017)

3.   Vassos Alexander, 'Running Up That Hill – The Highs and Lows of Going That Bit Further' (London: Bloomsbury Sport, 2018) which although it's structured around the Sparthalon across the Greek mainland also has some excellent chapters on UK races e.g. The Dragon's Back and South Downs Way 100. Vassos used an ABAB structure and inspired me with how well it lends itself to this kind of storytelling

4.   Adharanand Finn, 'The Rise of the Ultra Runners – A Journey to the Edge of Human Endurance' (London: Guardian Faber Publishing, 2019) which again does have some UK races as Adharanand builds up points for the Ultra-Trail Du Mont Blanc

5.   www.filmmyrun.com

6.   www.centurionrunning.com/races/thames-path-100-2020

7.   Joel Newton & Henry Stedman, 'Thames Path'(Hindhead: Trailblazer Publications, 2018), p.142.

8.   In Vybarr Cregan-Reid, 'Footnotes – How Running

Makes Us Human' (London: Ebury Press, 2016) there are some poetic sections on his relationship with the path as a runner e.g. p.167.

9.   Coincidentally this junction is just a few hundred metres along from the Lenham checkpoint at 91 miles in Centurion Running's North Downs Way 100

10.   I've found this book useful for mental techniques – Dr Jeff Brown with Liz Neporent, 'The Runner's Brain – How to think smarter to run better' (New York: Rodale Books,2015)

11.   Joel Newton & Henry Stedman, 'Thames Path' (Hindhead: Trailblazer Publications, 2018), p.193

12.   Andy Mouncey, 'So you want to run an ultra' (Marlborough: Crowood Press, 2014) p.19

13.   www.londonyouth.org

14.   Thames Path National Trail, Harvey Maps

15.   Vybarr Cregan-Reid, 'Footnotes – How Running Makes Us Human' (London: Ebury Press, 2016) pp.105-106

16.   Joel Newton & Henry Stedman, 'Thames Path' (Hindhead: Trailblazer Publications, 2018), pp.46,174

17.   Dr Tim Lomas, 'The Happiness Dictionary' (London: Piatkus, 2018) pp. 235-237

18.   Dean Karnazes, 'Ultra Marathon Man: Confessions of an All-Night Runner' (London: Allen & Unwin, 2017)

19.   Christopher Winn, 'I Never Knew That About The River Thames' (London: Ebury Press, 2010) p.112.

20.   Andy Mouncey, 'So you want to run an ultra' (Marlborough: Crowood Press, 2014)

21.   www.albionrunning.org/flat50

22.   Vybarr Cregan-Reid, 'Footnotes – How Running Makes Us Human' (London: Ebury Press, 2016) pp.96-98, quote from p.98

23.   Giacomo O.Squintani, 'Finding My Way' (Portishead: Amazon, 2016)

24.   Joel Newton & Henry Stedman, 'Thames Path' (Hindhead: Trailblazer Publications, 2018), p.148

25.   Andy Mouncey, 'So you want to run an ultra' (Marlborough: Crowood Press, 2014) p.80

26.   www.youtube.com/watch?v=Wh46k5yCaTs

27.   www.challenge-running.co.uk/races/stort30

28.   Andy Mouncey, 'So you want to run an ultra' (Marlborough: Crowood Press, 2014) p.81

29.   https://www.ultrarunningltd.co.uk/training-schedule/100-mile/100-mile-training-schedule

30.   Christopher Winn, 'I Never Knew That About The River Thames' (London: Ebury Press, 2010) p.71.

31.   Tim Noakes MD 'The Lore of Running' (Cape Town: Human Kinetics, 2002)

32.   Christopher Winn, 'I Never Knew That About The River Thames' (London: Ebury Press, 2010) p.73.

33.   Dr Tim Lomas, 'The Happiness Dictionary' (London: Piatkus, 2018) pp. 270-272, quote from p.271

34.   Christopher Winn, 'I Never Knew That About The River Thames' (London: Ebury Press, 2010) p.64.

35.   Andy Mouncey, 'So you want to run an ultra' (Marlborough: Crowood Press, 2014) p.81

36.   Christopher Winn, 'I Never Knew That About The River Thames' (London: Ebury Press, 2010) p.53.

37.   For example there is some evidence-based material on this in Tim Noakes MD 'The Lore of Running' (Cape Town: Human Kinetics, 2002)

38.   Dr Tim Lomas, 'The Happiness Dictionary' (London: Piatkus, 2018) pp. 46-47

39.   Tim Noakes MD 'The Lore of Running' (Cape Town: Human Kinetics, 2002)

40.   Mihaly Csikszentmihalyi, 'Flow: The Psychology of Happiness' (London: Penguin Random House, 2002)

41.   Ibid pp.58-67

42.   Ibid p. 62

43.   A haunting and eloquent film from New Zealand https://youtu.be/qwwIE0cSaniA

44.   Abraham H Maslow, 'Religions, Values and Peak-Experiences' (Ohio State University Press, 1964)

45.   Fraher, Amy L. 'Hero-making as a defense against the anxiety of responsibility and risk: A case study of US Airways Flight 1549' (Organisational and Social Dynamics, 11 (1)) pp.59

Printed in Great Britain
by Amazon